County Lines

County Lines

87 Minnesota Counties, 130 Minnesota Poets

Edited by

David Bengtson
Charmaine Pappas Donovan
Angela Foster
John Calvin Rezmerski

Loonfeather Press
Bemidji, Minnesota

Cover and book design: Mary Lou Marchand
Cover photograph: Charmaine P. Donovan

First Printing 2008
Printed in the United States of America
ISBN 978-0-926147-27-0

Loonfeather Press is a not-for-profit small press organized under
Section 501 (c) (3) of the United States Internal Revenue Code.

This project has been financed in part with funds provided by
the State of Minnesota through the Minnesota Sesquicentennial
Commission's Grants Program to the League of Minnesota Poets.

Loonfeather Press
PO Box 1212
Bemidji, Mn 56619

Dedication

Jonathan Swift asserted that great poets are like bees, who through their work give humankind honey for food and wax for candles—providing both Sweetness and Light. The League of Minnesota Poets dedicates this collection to two poets, Minnesotans from birth, who have not only sweetened and enlightened our lives, but who have through their skill and perseverance inspired new generations to seek higher levels of accomplishment. Maxine Kaiser Russell, of Brainerd, whose lively and passionate verse is widely published, is the most senior active member of the League. The late Jeanette Hinds, most recently residing in Rochester and Edina, is known nationally for her versatility and depth of feeling. Their poems continue to feed our minds and make our aspirations glow.

Table of Contents

Preface

Minnesota has a vibrantly large and various population of poets. Some have had long careers. Some have written only a few poems, and may never have been published before. Some write in sonnets or blank verse, and some in lists or rhapsodic prose. Some are performance poets or slam poets; others contend against bonds of privacy and intimacy. Some are very matter-of-fact while others blaze with rhetoric or crackle with surrealism. Some are concerned only with their own poems, others compelled to introduce everyone they know to as wide a range of poets as they can. We've got environmental poets, confessional poets, humorous poets, traditional poets, academic poets, political poets, politically incorrect poets, lovesick poets, Native American poets, immigrant poets, farmer poets, downtown poets, storytelling poets, lyric poets, naïve poets, famous Janes, unknown Joes . . . . Here's how they found their way into *County Lines*:

In 2007, Ed Brandt, editor of *The Minneapolis Muse*, past member of the League of Minnesota Poets, and honorary member of the Midwest Federation of Chaparral Poets, wrote to Charmaine Pappas Donovan, President of L.O.M.P. telling how he had come upon the Minnesota Genealogical Society's plan to participate in the Sesquicentennial, and decided to find a way for grassroots poets (distinguished from poets affiliated with academic and non-profit arts institutions) to participate. He had spoken to L.O.M.P. board member Susan Chambers, suggesting an anthology. Discussion among League leaders led Donovan to seek a grant from the Sesquicentennial Committee, and to contact Loonfeather Press about collaborating on the project. She recruited League members John Rezmerski and Angela Foster, and widely-published poet and educator David Bengtson was enlisted as a fourth member of the editorial committee.

Back in the mid-1970s, at a large-group poetry reading at the University of Minnesota (Morris), distinguished poet Robert Bly (now Minnesota Poet Laureate) observed that Minnesota's poetry scene was unlike that in most states. Rather than having its poets confined to a few major cities, Minnesota had a large variety of committed poets scattered all over the state. Bly suggested an anthology in which every Minnesota county would be represented by poems composed by residents of the counties or by visitors from other counties who had documented experiences related to counties in which they did not reside.

A few years before, Bly had instigated the founding of the Minnesota Writers' Publishing House, which published chapbooks of poetry selected by a rotating committee. Income from each new book would finance the printing of the next book. After the Morris event, many participants hoped that the MWPH would eventually publish the County Anthology. But logistical and organizational difficulties interfered, and after about fifteen years and only fifteen books (none of which was the anthology) the venture was abandoned.

But not forgotten. Periodically, poets would recall Bly's suggestion, and their faces would glow, then sputter into "yeah, but…"

When Donovan asked Rezmerski to serve as an editor, he mentioned Bly's idea, and in a flurry of emails and conversations among the editors, the county anthology idea was merged with the sesquicentennial theme. Before long, solicitations for manuscripts went out and submissions started to appear. Bly himself granted permission to use an early poem of his that is not as well known as it deserves to be.

Bengtson became our mapmaker and keeper of statistics, as well as our keenest judge of quality. He wouldn't let us select a poem just because it was a quick way to fill a spot on the map; every selection had to serve some principle. Foster was our point person, monitoring all the communications with poets and mailing copies of manuscripts. Donovan and Foster, both L.O.M.P. officers, helped us make contacts with League members for poems about particular counties. Rezmerski and Bengtson, both former educators and frequent attendees or hosts of readings, contacted acquaintances who were not League members. Each of us kept an eye out and a telephone handy to solicit the work of other Minnesota poets who had not yet submitted work. Inevitably, some eluded our notice, while others did not respond. Sometimes it seemed that the poems we needed just fell into our laps. Other times, researching our literary history, we had to labor harder. Rezmerski searched through back issues of magazines, old anthologies, and more newly published books and booklets, as well as checking libraries for clues to the career paths of poets who sometimes showed up as little-known geniuses, or sometimes turned out to be hacks or rhymesters with bloated reputations or creaky egos. So onward we searched, spurred by the will of Donovan, who did her best to keep us on task.

As far as possible, we aimed to be as true as we could to the full range of Minnesota poetry. We wanted to keep some samples of poetry of the past, but to concentrate on contemporary work rather than attempting a different version of Robert Hedin's excellent historical collection *Where One Voice Ends Another Begins* (Minnesota Historical Society Press). We selected some poems that reflected particular parts of Minnesota's history, including (for example) a temperance exhortation, poems about earlier wars, and poems from old issues of the League's official publication *The Moccasin* (including the issue commemorating Minnesota's Centennial). We privileged poems about people and their experiences, rather than poems that are purely descriptive or philosophical. We tried diligently (and not as satisfactorily as we would have liked) to represent Minnesotans' various communities, constituencies, and affiliations.

Many of our selected writers are present or past members of L.O.M.P., but we carefully strove to be fair to unaffiliated poets. Many of the poems we eventually rejected were also by League members. We were equally likely to select work by students as by their teachers. Some who submitted poems were attracted by our announcements in schools, arts organization newsletters, museums, and libraries. Some were encouraged by other poets who had seen their work. Others were personally invited by editors who knew that certain works of theirs would energize the volume. All of the editors got tips by word of mouth, or in one way or another just stumbled across valuable work. We kept in mind that we needed to cultivate an expansive gaze and to broaden our subject material. We selected poems that are intended to comfort or soothe, and poems that aim to disturb. We tried to demonstrate the truth of Ecclesiastes' claim that "there is nothing new under the sun," and also to take seriously the notion that everything, no matter how old, deserves to be examined anew. After all the effort our poets have devoted to those principles, by what right dare we deny them their place under that same sun? Let us provide for them something to like, something to laugh at, something with which to disagree, something to encourage their consciences, and something to honor their lives. To paraphrase America's greatest bard, Walt Whitman, the work of poets is to bring cheer to the oppressed and fear to the hearts of those who oppress them. We might add, to bring understanding to those who do not know that they are being made to live smaller and poorer lives than they have been able to recognize. The poet's language is the means by which our lives record our efforts while our hopes illumine our aspirations. We may labor and eat silently and alone, but only through words do we achieve community and dignity, only through lamentation do we transcend suffering, only through praise do we share in beauty, only in the speaking of love do we establish a home, a family, a state—whatever our language might be.

Thanks to Jim Northrup's request that we print a poem of his in Ojibwe, its native language, we decided also to include the Dakota Flag Song. Various tribal nations have Flag Songs and Honoring Songs used to open powwows. This national anthem of the Dakota people is an appropriate reminder that the peoples of Minnesota are joined by their sense of the common good. Northrup's "Dash Iskigamiziganin," is a poem about the activities involved in the sugar bush tradition. Northrup says that "it answers certain questions about the process and reasons why I make maple syrup. In Ojibwe the words dash just means and…. The word dash symbolizes the sap coming out of the tree." A fitting end-piece for our collection, it depicts the work and joy of a community activity that is all at once ceremonial, playful, and practical, and in which everyone can play a role—not unlike the making of an anthology, which is a kettle of syrup to be shared.

We sought poems that deal with a wide range of experiences typical of Minnesota's diverse subcultures, occupations, and activities, including local celebrations, fishing, burdens of life and subsistence, agonies and humiliations to which people are subjected, and the varieties of weather. Don't look here for "Gee, my county is pretty" poems, or panegyrics to religious benevolence, or sentimental goo about "Weren't things just about perfect back when Grandma still had the farm?" The world shows us pain and conflict, danger and love, greed and generosity, whimsy and "homeland security", pride and prejudice, television and loud mufflers, and "Yeah, but …" And so do our poems. Not everyone will agree with all of our selections—often we disagreed among ourselves about *why* we chose one poem rather than another. We hope that you will find much here to stimulate your consciousness, and that *County Lines* will pay out lines that connect you with your ancestors and your neighbors. We hope you will find in the crafted words of your neighbors something that will help our state endure, and deserve its endurance, for centuries to come.

County Lines

Prologue

WAPAHA ODOWAN

(Dakota Flag Song, traditional)

Tunkansidan yapi,
tawapaha kin han.
Owihanke sni he nazin kte do.

Iyohdateya oyate kin han,
wicicage kta ca,
decamon wedo.

(Their grandfathers'
flag will stand
waving forever.

Underneath it
the people will grow,
so I do this to honor it.)

— Aitkin County —

Jane Levin

Odd Girl Out

Grandville, Minnesota,
where Larsens marry the Larsons
who sat behind them in homeroom,
their connection more contagion
than attraction.

Unmarried girls leave.
Tomboys, who grew up in foxholes
to escape friendly ire, don't tell.

No one asks.

Gordon Prickett

Too Many People

Alone on this early street?
A COUGH! across the way says no.

Like Hong Kong in 1991, there are people moving
on this Oakland street at every hour.

Running, walking, walking dogs, running with leashed dogs
or no leash, cycling, motoring, on sidewalk, roadway, driveway
close by each other.

The houses fill up their 50 by 50 foot lots
with cars left at the curb.

Any garages are scarce space for storage
and spillover living.

Regulations and permits tell you when to move your car,
scoop after your pets, cross the street with ...7, 6, 5, 4 more seconds
to get out of the way.

From the northwoods of Minnesota I came for a few weeks.
Today I fly back and resume life in winter as we know it.

We who portage, paddle, plow, fish, and hunt
grow food, build things, mine ore, cut timber, raise cattle

don't drink so much wine
or insist on so many kinds of coffee.

My country road has more deer than settlers.
No wonder the absence of quiet leads me to see

a future diminished by too many people.

(At Noah's New York Bagels in Oakland, California,
7:10 a.m., Monday, January 7, 2008)

— Anoka County —

Marianne McNamara

Laundry Day

Ma washed on Mondays,
heavy cotton sheets, towels
and fancy embroidered pillowcases
strung out to dry on the old rope
between the oak and sugar maple in our yard.

A brown-eyed baby balanced on one hip,
bursting laundry basket with tiny socks

poking through frayed willow holes on the other,
wooden clothespins stowed in her apron pocket
and one or two stuck in her mouth like straight pins
porcupining from a pincushion.

The maple was a good climbing tree
and while Ma tacked up dripping bedclothes
I'd scramble to my lookout post,
the skipper navigating swirling grass green seas.
The breeze billowed the sun-bleached sheets,
flapped and filled them like sails on a schooner,

whipped make-believe waves into meringue whitecaps,
collided them over and over against the sandy shore.
Best of all was the sweet smell of the bedclothes
when Ma unpegged the wind-dried sails
and tucked them back on our beds.

Jana A. Bouma

The Famous Anoka Potato

"The Minnesota potato is considered the best potato raised."
-The New York Times, September 25, 1903

I wonder if he laid them here, old Reuel Hall, these worn bricks, this remnant of a wall. He knew better than to listen to those Boston bankers. He knew to buy a ticket, to ride the train across the Ohio and north along the Mississippi. As he passed Lake Pepin, he already saw the belts flying and the drive shafts turning, the maw of the grater devouring the clean-washed russets, the wagons laboring toward St. Paul, carrying the pure, shining starch to kitchens and laundries across the young continent.

He knew potato country when he saw it—the sandy soil where plump tubers would burst from the earth, ready for the bins, for the troughs and the washers, ready to form that pulpy slurry, the snowy granules in the rivers of water.

The vines sent up their purple flowers. The farmers filled their carts. Wives on Saturday left spacious kitchens to come to town, to spend their potato money on gingham and glass and sweet molasses. The talk at the local tavern was all the potato. The city council kept its eye on the potato. The mayor watched the laborers with their shovels and their wheelbarrows, smoothing the new road to carry the potato. When twenty years had passed, they gathered, every one, to toast old Reuel Hall, who sat before them, smiling that gracious, distant smile. They knew to put their trust in the potato.

Old Reuel Hall rests today beneath a distant stone. The corn stands tall, the beans hang heavy, here, above the sandy soil. A warm, starchy redolence has settled from the air. The Pearson boys cast their eyes down rows of corn, calculating bushels and futures. Their father stands here, too, and remembers his father, driving down the long, straight rows on the old Allis-Chalmers.

They look across this field and do not see, not one of them, the purple flowers nodding in the early June sun.

— Becker County —

Stash Hempeck

First Kill

Dusk
slips silent
across the lead-lined sky.

Like the
              slow sway
of a fall's
              last leaf

your family
ghosts
across the road and
onto the field

—delicate like a dancer almost—
silent
in your brown and white
camouflage.

You bend head and body
down low.
Another follows
then a second
and a third
until all twelve
graze lightly forward over the earth.

As I scope that ground—soundless—
you—unafraid—
rise up
to meet my gaze.

And across that distance,
through that hollow tube of almost night,
our eyes lock—aware.

And when you blink

I softly breathe out my forgiveness
—clasp it solid against my thanks—
before I gently squeeze the trigger.

Bob La Fleur

Yes, I Don't Fish

A fish jumps with perfect aim, flops
and settles over a bed of herbs, spices,
and chopped onions.

The fire
by this time is belching red hot, coaling,
turning silent and white. The skillet

is cast iron, seasoned with seasoned
imaginings.

Yes, I don't fish.
I don't even imagine that I fish.
I open the freezer door, take out
a walleye, thaw and slap it in a pan,
add a little of this, a little of that,
cook up some wild rice, sit by the fire.

Though I fall asleep there
and dream, I never dream I fish.
And I don't imagine other fish
to be like this fish—until
my hunger returns, then each
in its turn, as it thaws, reminds me
of the catch I didn't catch, the stories
I have no need to tell.

— **Beltrami County** —

Diane Glancy

March 21, 2005, The Shootings at Red Lake Reservation, Red Lake, Minnesota

It was the dreams.

They came like arrows. Sometimes I woke remembering
something long ago. Other times I knew I only dreamed.
Sometimes I heard the hiss of an arrow hitting its mark—
SCHWUUUUUUUPP!!
It was something I wanted to hear again. I slept hoping I would dream.

It was the aquarium light I watched at school.
I think the fish called to me there.

The dreams hid when the nightmares came.
The fish sat on the bed. He said not to be afraid. He asked if I was
hungry. I opened my mouth.
I heard a car. My father came in. He sobbed in his bed. He slept.
I woke in the morning crying.
Shut up, my father says. He has worries—He has things that take him
from me—
My father was defeated.
He killed himself—shot himself in the head.

There was a fish inside me growling.

I cried but she did not hear—My mother's mouth moved—
She slept with her large eye open on the side of her head.
She swam on the highway. She slid off the road.
I was in the room. They were talking to me.
Someone would stay with me.
They were outside talking.
No one heard the fish.
I cried but they didn't hear.
My mother was in an accident—Driving while drunk.
Would she die?
There was blackness in the house. The moving voices there.
Frogs. Snakes. Creeping things I felt around my ankles.
But a fish doesn't have ankles.
Then neither did I.

No one remembered I was there.
I looked for something to eat. There was nothing.
I felt the fish in my stomach and was not hungry.
If I could hunt, I would shoot a squirrel. I would kill a fox.
I would eat them whole.

Sometimes a river moves in me. It is swimming with awful things.
My mother will not be home.
She doesn't know me. She is not herself. She is a ghost.
She has gone somewhere.
There is someone who looks like a mother. But she is not.
The fish knows it too.
We talk about who she is. We know it is not her.
We look for my mother in the river. The fish does not find her.

I was a bottom feeder. I was nothing.
Anger choked me. It caught my fin in its trap.
The world was heavy. It was bleeding.
I was a throw away.
I tried to find a footing, but always slipped back.
No one cared.
I was stupid.
They set up rules. I could never understand.

My mother never came back.
I heard those rodents in the walls of the house.
I knew when I slept on my bones.
Those rabbits I caught and poked a stick into—Let them squirm.
Let them know what it is to hurt.

The teachers said I was trouble. No one stood up for me.
Everyone said I was trouble. What would they do with me?

I went into the river. I lived with fish.
They would not find me there.
I visited my mother in the hospital. She was in her own hell.
The fish said my mother was sorry she was the way she was.
It was her spirit that left—
It got up and went away, and left her the way she was.

I wanted to shoot myself—
I would take others with me—
The fish? More than the fish.
Everyone who left me underwater.
I tried to swim away, but could not.
I was in the school's homebound program for violation of school policy.
I posted messages on a neo-Nazi website.
Signed myself *Todesengel,* German for angel of death.
Wasn't it the Nazis who used the 7th Cavalry Indian extermination policy
and murdered Jews the same as the cavalry massacred Indians?
This cloudy logic.
This murky underwater.
This taking on enemy clothes.

Now the fish was in the aquarium light of the computer.

The screen glowed in the dark room.
My eyes moved on line in REM sleep reading the screen.
I entered a river in which death could—what?
The nightmares hunted me.
I felt their teeth.
I felt my eyes swim like a fish.

I planned a raid with my friends.
We would blow them away—Drive like warriors over the land.
Our names would be known.
We would bring hell into this *dull*—
We would be legend.
My eyes swam through our e-mails.

Where's the hook to pull the fish out?
There is none—None.
I would kill the world.

It was purpose. It was buzz. It was the hunt.
They had taken our world placed theirs over ours and said it was
ours now too.
We were underwater now.
The hook was in our mouth.
We connected by e-mail. It was power. It was grace.

The school put me out.
I felt the warrior blood.
The urge to war—To prove myself a warrior fish.

The fish said I could kill.
The others wouldn't come with me.

It was cold—my grandmother's house where I lived.
The fish called me underwater. His fins moved like waves on the screen.
The fish taught me to hold a rifle.
He said he did not have arms.
He was a fish and I could hold the rifle for him.

I went to my grandfather's house—Killed him and his girlfriend.
Took his shotgun and walked into school.

I blasted my way into Red Lake High School past the metal detector.

Killed the security guard.
Killed a teacher, students,
wounded others with two hand guns and my grandfather's shotgun.

I blew them away—
They didn't know I was coming.
They weren't looking for a fish—

The water in the aquarium parted and I passed through.

I shot myself or someone did in the shoot-out.
No, I shot myself after I had been shot.

A fish swells with rage.
A fish grows arms.
A fish lurches forward.
A fish holds a gun.

Doris Lueth Stengel

Wilderness of Welcome

I came to Beltrami County as a bride
to a someplace called Saum. Not much
here except my husband's kinfolk.
My small nuclear family suddenly
exploded into cousins by the dozens.
Each quarter mile another farm, another relative,
or near-relative, for even those not related
hailed from the same cold valley in Norway.

Proud monuments had been erected here:
a log school my mother-in-law attended,
nearby a two story white-painted building
reputed to be the first consolidated
school in northern Minnesota.
A mile away stands the spired
Tolgen Lutheran Church
with its skirt of graves, tidily mowed.

My eyes accustomed to the heroic sky
of North Dakota, to sunset-filled horizons
now cutoff, I was blinded by trees.
Storms leaped out from bushes.

My idea of a farm was hundreds of acres
of wheat or oats or blue-flowered flax.
These 40 acre plots of spruce swamp
provided slim living—a few cows,
pigs, and chickens.

Yet these skimpy, brushy acres
produced a community of stubborn-strong
families who sent young men to war,
who shared their meager resources,
who embraced a Dakota girl
with arms wide as a prairie.

Patricia Conner

You Don't Have To Write Him A Sonnet

Only note
that his lashes
beg to be stroked
like the pelt
of a hound.
Observe
the curve of his body:
sleek power.
Describe the dive
of an eagle,
the sparkle
of glass.
Discover
granite outcroppings:
white rock
thrust up
into meadows. Consider
the softness
of grass.

— Benton County —

Claire van Breemen Downes

House on the Bluff

(For Neil Baird Thompson, whose house sat on the county line)

I remember the day you showed us
      the trail left by the ox-carts.
We stood by the white picket fence behind your house
     and you   gleeful as a boy displaying
his prize arrowhead   pointed them out.
      There   in the narrow
    disused easement they lay   sharp-cleft
under the dobby green   too deep
      for a century to obliterate.
And of a sudden in the autumn afternoon
    I could see the wagons lurching down
       to the Mississippi   hear the
       creak and the rattle   the snap
       of the whip   the shouts
    smell the dust   the sweat   the dung.

Winter has fallen upon us.
The frozen river lies white.
The picket fence is drifted over.
The tracks are hidden.

Cut so deep.
Spring will uncover them again
whether anyone looks or not.

— Big Stone County —

Robert Bly

In a Boat on Big Stone Lake

for Jack Maguire

I

How beautiful it is, aging, to be out with friends
On the water! Already, in June,
The water heavy with green filaments
Of life. Spring birds send in a warning
From the South Dakota shore.

II

The briefness of life! How the yellow rope
Shines in the water-walking sun!
From inside us, deep ages
Walk across the water, buildings
Fall, the angel has spread its wings
Over the dark valley of tiny minutes.

III

The country staggers toward light-hearted brutality.
We have made a long journey
And no one knows who is coming back.
I remember the muskrat's head, so sleek,
I remember something floating on the water.

— Blue Earth County —

Susan Stevens Chambers

Bill the Farm Hand

When Grandfather ventured from his fjords
luck tossed him to the north side of this state.
He chose a claim there although settlers
spoke of richer soils south.
He and Pa attacked the land:
struck trees, hefted rocks.
Our neighbor Sven took one look at their size,
cussed the glaciers, and turned
out dairy cows to shadow between trees.

Pa and Grandfather laughed at him.
They marked their days off with sweat,
heaving boulders and a growing pain down their spine.
Each time they opened a field it grew more rocks.
Grandfather, staggered in the flax—
heart turned granite—fell and rolled into the rock pile.
Sven prospered.

My father bent over those stones. He cursed,
watched meager grain shrivel in the sand.
One day they were too big.
He walked away from the farm
  the mortgage,
   the other kids and me,
    he walked away from Ma.

She said I would slip away, too.
When she lost the farm I tried to stay,
but I hated the place in town. I drifted south,
avoiding cities. I searched for stoneless living.
So I came to work for the Carlsons.
This county tastes of black soil:

I work the entire field and never
turn a rock. The Carlsons are good people.
But sometimes, while perched high
on the bins working the corn downward
like Sven's daughter shaking out her hair,
I wonder if the Carlsons know
that their prosperity rests so much
 on stones,
            rain,
                luck and the choices
                        their grandfather made.

Cary Waterman

Getting My Son

You've been gone a week.
Your feet are larger and cannot be side-stepped.
And your head is smaller than I remember it.
Your voice is different too.
I have never heard it before
and I tumble between the words
the way a river runs downhill,
loving the stone of the rapids,
and loving the way the moss clings to everything.

While you were gone
my fingernails grew twice as long.
And I discovered the spaces around my heart.
While you were gone
I found a new voice to speak with.
There are silences now between my words
that defy swimming.

The land between Mankato and Blue Earth burns with August.
And driving to get you I sloped downhill like the harvest,
all the way to your grandfather
and to his cheerfulness at having made it through the week.

Your grandmother has you spit-shined.
Your curls are gone.
And in the short walk of one week
we have left and come back together
like two explorers with a rendezvous
at the mouth of the river.

Philip S. Bryant

Polka Dancing Televised Live From Mankato on Saturday Night

A dairy farmer all the way from Albany, Minnesota, and
his very fat wife danced to
the polka She's Too Fat for Me
laughing and singing along with
the words, holding each other
tight in one another's arms.
He twirled her like she was
some willowy dark-eyed Russian ballerina singing
into her ear like a teenager
in love for the first time
in his life,
"You can have
her, I don't want her, she's too
fat for me, she's too fat for me"—lifting her off her
feet high into the air
and setting her 300 pound frame down
as lightly as you would
set a newborn babe in her crib at night.
In response to him
she throws her head
back tango style—
and gives out a raucous
rose between the teeth laugh
as he starts in on
another chorus of the
She's Too Fat for Me Polka
before giving her another one of his now patented
death defying twirls.

Cary Waterman

Raising Lambs

for Ron and Ann Gower

The lambs push their honey-lips into the grass.
Each one wears a dangly red earring
that tells us shots have been given,
balls castrated,
that the long arm of ownership
has clamped its staple.
They are so small against the spring,
three of them clustered
on a field of green baize
like card players who care more
for companionship than the win or loss.
Black on soft noses,
sooty legs lost in grass.
These are the no-name sheep,
wethers going in a mud-scented June evening
toward their short plump existence.

We move into the house and have lamb for dinner.
Succulent, smeared with mint and garlic,
rainbows of juice in the pockets of our cheeks.
What a fine testimony to this grass, this earth,
to those nursery rhyme loves who will never know
how we have each wished under a full summer moon
to fall on all fours and tear the grass,
to lap water from a cold stone trough,
and to live frivolous all through one summer
before marching full-blooded, red-hearted into fall
toward the butcher's swing of steel,
his unfailing arms which embrace,
take hold and love us
until we know none of it anymore.

— Brown County —

Nancy Paddock

Heritagefest

The sunburned man is serious
about the chicken dance.
He flaps his elbows, shifts his hips, clucks
earnestly in this canopy of patriotic color,
this glow of old polkas and schottisches,
harvest beer, and rocking, arm-locked rows
of American bodies.

The imported band shouts in German.
Is answered in German. Hands clap in time;
sunlight halos bobbing heads.
Twenty-year-olds with babies
pass a pitcher along a table
littered with bratwurst and kraut, sweet hot
potato salad. Old women in tatted aprons
and folk-embroidered black dresses
smile benevolently at girls and boys swooping
round and round in the old time dance.

Three pants-suited women in a row
of couples near the door link arms, sway
tentatively in time with the oom-pa-pa.
One bumps, for a few measures,
into her immovable
husband and then stands still.

Soft, flush-faced old men in gray lederhosen
and red suspenders sit stiffly clapping.
One has risen. White hair flying,
blue eyes fixed on something only he can see,
he slaps his heavy palms together
through every song.

— Carlton County —

Katharine Johnson

Fresh Brookies

Pa had more fish stories
than he could ever tell
on a single below-zero winter night.
After steamy sauna
we sat around
the green oil-clothed table.
We ate cardamom bread
dunked in coffee thick with cream
and listened to fish tales.

I grew up picking bones from pike
while listening to how the fish bit the hook.
How the rod bent almost double.
How a perch leapt right into the boat.
How the big one got away.

One morning, years later,
Pa called me.
"Fresh Brookies," he said.

I drove as fast as I dared
wondering about this old man,
my father,
who tramped through boggy ground
and tangles of alder brush
to get to his favorite fishing hole
at so early an hour.

Pa piled my plate at the stove with trout,
fresh from the stream
and hot out of the fry pan.
That day there was no fish story.

All he said was, "Eat now. Fresh Brookies."

Jim Northrup

Shrinking Away

Survived the war but was having
Trouble surviving the peace
Couldn't sleep more than two hours
Was scared to be without a gun
Nightmares, daymares, guilt and remorse
Wanted to stay drunk all the time
1966 and the VA said Vietnam wasn't a war
They couldn't help but did give me
A copy of the Yellow Pages
Picked a shrink off the list
50 bucks an hour
I was making 125 a month
We spent six sessions establishing rapport
I heard about his military life, his homosexuality
His fights with his mother, and anything
Else he wanted to talk about
At this rate we would have got to me in 1999
Gave up on that shrink
Couldn't afford him, wasn't doing me any good
Six weeks later my shrink killed himself
Great
Not only guilt about the war
But new guilt about my dead shrink
If only I had a better job
I could have kept on seeing him
I thought we were making real progress
Maybe in another six sessions
I could have helped him
I realized then that
Surviving the peace
Was up to me.

Jim Northrup

Ogichidaa

I was born in war, WW Two
Listened as the old men told stories
Of getting gassed in the trenches, WW One
Saw my uncles come back from
Guadalcanal, North Africa, and the
Battle of the Bulge
Memorized the war stories
My cousins told of Korea
Felt the fear in their voices
Finally it was my turn
My brothers too
Joined the Marines in time
For the Cuban Missile Crisis
Heard the crack of rifle fire
In the rice paddies south of Danang
Then tasted the bitterness of the only war
America ever lost
My son is now a warrior
Will I listen to his stories
Or cry into his open grave

— Carver County —

Mike Hazard

Flying Colors

while my birding buddies look aloft
in the budding branches and blue skies
listening for songs of a feather,
I linger among the green long grasses
loaded with dew, chanting silently

"debauchee of dew, debauchee of dew"
when zooming in closer I realize,
at a thousand points of view,
with tiny motions of my eyes,
each bead of water shoots a new
firework of colored light,
a mirror of birds in flight:
red cardinal, orange oriole,
yellow flicker, green head mallard,
blue-winged warbler, indigo bunting,
black and white tern …
we pause with our binoculars,
mesmerized as we try to memorize
the tiny song of a sparrow
we cannot see or name for sure:
grasshopper? Baird's? Henslow's?
somewhere over the rainbows
a song of a tiny sparrow
calls us across the meadow

— Cass County —

Michael Dennis Browne

Evensong

"There he is" he learns to say
when we glimpse the great sun burning down
toward the hill, and "There she is"
when we spot the pale enormous moon
floating low above the pines;
and over and over, swiveling his head,
he says it as I drive them both,
daughter and son, around the roads
until they sleep, so I can have
dinner and an hour alone with their mother.

Ahead in the shadows, two deer.
A little further, metal abandoned
in somebody's yard, auto parts
and ancient appliances, that later
the moon will make into something,
that same skilled stranger keeping us
company beyond the branches.

He wants to know why they share the sky,
and all I can tell him is it's a secret
we have to guess at as we go;
and "There he is" he says once more
as the hill prepares to swallow fire,
and "There she is" as she climbs the air,
and murmurs and murmurs until he sleeps
(and she already is sleeping).

Doris Bergstrom

Winter Collection

A drop of sun
hovers on the horizon,
slides southward
farther, faster
earlier each day.
People who forsake the northland
keep their distance from snow boots,
comforter, scarf,
fruit soup, lutefisk.

Sun wants gratuities—
tales of the Moon
a society of stars
winter constellations
music in the night
clouds.

We who wait want it all.

— Chippewa County —

Phebe Hanson

Wrestler

You retired early from the Lutheran ministry,
had plenty of time on your hands, only 62,
with stored-up energy from sitting
for so many years, reading the Bible and writing sermons,
so you began to add apartments to your house
on Edgcumbe Road, turning the basement
into a one-bedroom complete with functioning fireplace,
although you were rather testy when tenants actually used
the fireplace, something you never did with the one
in your living room, preferring to keep it smoke and ash free,
and you converted the attic
into a snug efficiency, providing rental income
in your declining years, although you were not declining,
still did substitute preaching, always tape-recording your sermons,
always inviting me into your study to listen to them, even though
I objected: "I'd rather just sit and talk to you, dad."

You also took to watching professional wrestling on TV.
How strange to see you absorbed in images of writhing male flesh,
you who had denied me in childhood the pleasures of movies,
calling them carnal and immoral.

So today I am shopping at Gary's Red Owl—
they try to make the impersonal chains sound humanly-owned here
in Montevideo, Minnesota—and as I wheel
my cart slowly down every aisle on a desultory quest
for groceries I don't really need, my heart is suddenly gladdened
by the sight of a red school folder. It's THE HULKSTER
in tight electric blue trunks, massive shoulders and torso oiled
    and bronzed,
a World Wrestling Federation champion, holding
an enormous trophy, strategically placed to not quite cover his crotch,

and I buy the folder for you, father, whose flesh must by now
be mostly gone inside your casket. You'd instructed us to pick
the cheapest one there was, but the mortician said, "This one
is too small for Reverend Dale. He was a husky man, you know.
His shoulders are too broad to fit," and I realized for the first time
you had a body of flesh and blood, a body built like a wrestler's.

— Chisago County —

Marjorie Buettner

Day after day, throughout the winter,
We hardened ourselves to live by bluest reason
In a world of wind and frost …
                    —Wallace Stevens

Three Sijo:

1.
all day long and into the night
this world changed by snowfall
and under sound the howling wind
like a wounded animal
I turn off the light and settle in bed
wanting only you

2.
there is a deer galloping in my backyard
    this early dawn
and eagles hover silently
    over the open lake

even I at odd times fly
    and leap into the unknown

3.
the lake becomes its own landscape
   wintertide washing in
the air transforms to crystal flowers
   this snow-gathering wind
here in a world of one color
   the sound no sound makes

Jane Levin

Devotion

ten little blue stems at sunset
the minyan stands tall
bends in unison
wispy heads bob to earth
then sky
       then earth again
whiskers quivering
          East

— Clay County —

Thom Tammaro

Closing the Cabin

1.

In the yawn of dusk,
we drift home in Minnesota autumn,
reciting the litany once more:
dock in; boat house latched;
rugs rolled; plugs pulled;
windows hinged; floors swept;

pilots out; pipes drained;
faucets opened; doors locked;
hummingbird feeder taken down;
key hanging in its secret place.

2.

In the flicker of lights near the city's edge
we talk easily, gather within
all that the summer has given:
a great fish, slender and shiny,
diving for bottom; loons calling
in the still afternoon;
stars swirling above the rooftops.
Near home, vees of geese circle,
circle in the shadows above us.

3.

Later that night, we pause
on the stairs—winterward—
unlock that other season
where little puffs of winter dust
rise when we open the door.

Mark Vinz

Homesteaders

When they came
some of them already knew
that here was more than flatness;
here at last was a place
where all things would be possible.

       * *

Call it ocean, call it desert;
trails move off in all directions—

tall grass, wheatfield, open range.
Everyone here is traveler.
No one knows the way.

* *

The buffalo wallow is thick with prairie aster,
coneflower, gentian, blazing star.
We walk the fields till dusk,
when deer come down to drink at the river
and a cool wind ruffles the bluestem.
The sky is full of old bones.

Mark Vinz

Red River Valley

From time to time, there comes a need to
drive the backroads, past meandering streams
we didn't expect, the tiny graveyards
and falling-down sheds, the lone trees
plowed around so carefully.
In a place this flat and endless,
each small variation seizes the eye.
The car tracks eastward to the gradual rise
of glacial beaches. Beyond are hills
with woods and lakes, but we turn north
along the valley's edge, a broad horizon
cradling clouds, and then to the west,
past land that holds a dozen different
kinds of hay bales. Not far from home
by country reckoning we stop beside
a field edged with a swath of zinnias—
a quarter mile of blossoms, bright-headed
in waning light. It's getting late, but
still we watch the flowers—what we
won't forget those last dark miles
where other lights come out to meet us.

Thom Tammaro

Thinking of Steinbeck and Charley

I am traveling west on U.S. 10, the old east-west highway that originally connected Minneapolis-St. Paul to the rest of the state, long before the clean, pale concrete path of I-94 ribboned its way across the Minnesota landscape. Along U.S. 10, the tiny towns of western Minnesota unfold—Audubon, Hawley, Glyndon, Dilworth—inviting the unhurried traveler to pause, to linger in their diners or what my good friend calls their "Loneliness Cafes," to eat American Road Food, to sip steaming coffee from worn and chipped eggshell-colored cups before resuming their 65 miles-per-hour-life. I am traveling west of the same highway Steinbeck and Charley traveled as they moved through Dacotah Territory in early October of 1960. Fargo is still in the crease in the map, and I suspect the crease itself is the Red River. I, too, have stopped and talked with people in some of the restaurants where they might have stopped, though perhaps they weren't named "Willy's" or "Highway Host" or "The Silver Spike" back then. And instead of debating whether baked donuts float, we talk of secret bends in the Buffalo River where northern pike and walleye wait for us. And I have eaten homemade sausage purchased from a roadside stand along this same road. Steinbeck was right: you do leave flame-red maple country and head toward flame-yellow birch. And yes, there are farms tucked into the rolling hills not far from Detroit Lakes where 10,000 turkeys flow across the landscape like white water. There are stretches of U.S. 10 where I have stopped in early October to see 3,000 Canadian geese vee south, and in winter, coming back from ice fishing, I have paused along these frozen stretches to gaze at Northern lights spilling and pulsating cornflower blue and sea green along the northern prairie horizon. In summer, traveling U.S. 10, heading home from the Lakes region where I've had some luck with northern pike and bass, little with walleye, I usually check the rear view mirror, glance toward the campgrounds and the parking lots of bars that line the main streets of these tiny towns, hoping to glimpse a pickup truck with a camper top, the shadow of a tall, slim figure at the wheel, the faint outline of a dog riding shotgun. I think I've seen them once or twice. It's always before I reach a town's edge, before the K-Mart and Pizza Hut; before the Dairy Queen and electronic arcade; before the carpet warehouses and furniture discount center. It's always dusk, the light going from gray to black, streaks of cobalt and dusty rose mingling and fading into prairie night. Rising from a dip, they're coming from the last of the glacial mounds before the valley flattens and spreads itself to North Dakota. I slow down and let them pass. I nod. I follow the glow of their ruby taillights into the Minnesota night. The stars unfolding, I think of prophets and prophecy.

— Clearwater County —

David Bengtson

The Cows Nearly Make It

He's heading back to town. Ahead of him on the right shoulder, something is moving, something big. He slows down and sees that it's a cow, a Holstein, wait a minute, there's another one in front of it, and another, they're running. 13, 14, 15, 16, he keeps counting, driving slowly. He hits the high beams and sees them stretched out as far as the light reaches, an entire herd of Holsteins hoofing it from their farm to town on the shoulder of Highway 92. 37, 38, 39, 40, 41. In the distance, lights are flashing. 50, 51, 52.

Tomorrow, in the paper, he'll read how the cows wandered off a farm about fourteen miles south of town and were stopped nearing the city limits at 2:40 a.m. A patrol dispatcher will say, "I think we found some of the fastest cows in the state."

As he gets closer, he sees police cars and pickups parked on the other shoulder. 64, 65, 66, 67. Police and others scatter across the highway and ditch, waving their arms and flashlights at the leaders of the herd. 78, 79, 80.

They are two miles from the city limits. Who knows what would have happened if they hadn't been stopped? 81. If they had gotten all the way to town? 82. Two more miles, that's all they had left! 83. And they could have made it! 84.

— Cook County —

Freya Manfred

The Glowing Brown Snails of Blueberry Lake

The first time I dive under water
and open my eyes near shore
I see the glowing brown snails
of Blueberry Lake.
Shaggy mussels too,
that pump themselves shut
when I touch their soft lips.
And old sticks, soggy and twisted,
wriggling like water snakes
through rust-soft, leathery reeds.
And acorns, worn creamy white
in the constant waves, caught
between rocks and pebbles:
pink, brown, green, and blue.
And one gray stone
with the black and white print
of a maple leaf
stamped on it forever
by the press of winter ice.

Kay Grindland

Cataract

Wind shows river
how to fly down the mountain,
teaches grass how to ambush the ground,
the lake far below
how to scurry away.

I hold fast to the old bridge
as water rushes beneath,
as the gale roars through,
I practice how to lean into anything.

Wind tears a birch limb down,
I toss a stick into the foam.

Some things I've lost,
but the ways I've left
to answer this day
would busy the wind forever.

Kay Grindland

Plunge

If, in the morning,
you wake early,
think of me diving from granite
into blue water.

The gasp of cold
kisses my skin awake
by drop, by deluge,
lake like muscle enfolds me,
soft wrap of blood-warmed water.

I rise and lift each cell into springy air,
wetness spills onto sun-baked rock,
a quiver of cold dances each hair awake.

I think of you
as your shirt drops its soft weight down
to capture my warmth.

Old flannel,
muscled water,

quickening chill,
    heat seeping,
christening air,
affection,

I wear you all at once.

— Cottonwood County —

Winifred M. Hoppert

Red Rock Church

The prairie flat
Is like a floor of tile
Or wood;
No softness there to break
The line
And each protrusion
Visible for miles
From size and height and conformation
Reveals its identity.
Each village, each town,
Is dominated and located
By its cluster of elevators
To mark its place against the sky.
What delight and surprise
To find in the middle of all that flatness
The spire and stretch
Of a country church!
The churchyard may be circled …
Like the fringe of gray hair
Edging a bald head …
By its own history written
On tombstones in its private yard.
Softened by ancient lilacs
In a prairie spring,

In prairie winter
The church will stand
Buffeted by winds with cruel chill
Or other times drenched by rains which pelt
The bricks.
The parish worshipping within that church
Has itself been shaped and formed
By those same winds and rains,
Assaulted by the sweet compelling
Perfume from lilacs in their season.
Sturdy men and women
Sincere, kind despite the harshness
Of the prairie winter,
They have attested to the strength
Of their faith
By rearing here a spire
Pointing to the God
Who from His Heaven
Gives them "their meat in due season
And satisfieth the desire of every living thing."

— Crow Wing County —

Doris Lueth Stengel

At the Clothesline

I lift my arms
to hang a pillowcase.
My face turned upward
warms in daffodil sun.

On the birch crown
a cardinal whistles

for his mate,
while the neighbor's cat
glides through grass
tail twitching.

I stoop, grasp corners
of a sheet, pin one end,
another pin midway
and one at hem.
The sheet fills with April,
a landlocked sail.

The condominium complex
nearby forbids clotheslines,
depriving residents
of this ancient ritual,
this bending and reaching
humble and praising,
usurping their right
to rest in beds fragrant
with a hint of resurrection.

Candace Simar

Devil in the Details

When I think of small town life I get that smothery feeling, like swallowing feathers or eating too many marshmallows at once. It's that claustrophobic closeness I experience at family reunions or when Cousin Rodney cheerfully announces he will stay an extra two weeks. I know there are those who enjoy living in small towns but I think they are the ones linked to wonderful success. Like having a brother-in-law who played in the NFL or being the daughter of the 1941 Winter Carnival Queen. Such people don't have things in their lives they'd like to forget. But it's different if you are the one remembered for failing kindergarten or throwing up during the Christmas pageant or growing up the child of drunkards. These handicaps follow you to the grave. Like the thought of being naked in a crowd, exposed beyond comfort, no place to hide. Instinctively I clutch my rags of individuality closer so others can't ferret out the details. Sometimes I toss out the red herring, hint that this year I'll vote Green or that I'm considering yoga classes; anything to throw them off the scent. But in a small town you can't escape. Everyone knows everything about you and your family and your kids and your great uncle and your third cousin. Nothing sacred. Nothing forgotten. It's been said the devil is in the details. The devil must feel at home in small towns. At least the ones I have known.

Maxine Russell

Hangman's Tree

Near the Last Turn Saloon, Brainerd, Minnesota

I just happened to be around those years
        too late or too soon
        however it all came about
I remained the last tree uncut
        no ragged crows would brush
        against my trunk   no leaves left
only a few barkless branches on me
    big enough for hanging men without trial
    strong enough for justice denied
by the posse in front of the Last Turn Saloon

I just happened to be the one
        used for a hangman's tree
        the noosed ropes with snapped necks
        creaking like a swing
my rotting roots puddled with blood
    then the bodies were cut down
I'd say around the hour of evening
    when the old harlot sun uncorked herself
    and sank into the ground
like red wine from a broken bottle

Joan Wiesner

The Lesson

In June I began teaching a raccoon poetry. It was hard work. While most of us hold an attention span of around twenty seconds, his lasted as long as it took him to eat a full ear of corn. For weeks I stuffed his ravenous appetite with sweet kernels, Shakespeare and Yeats. The raccoon devoured his food, all the while looking at me in a curious manner when I read aloud "In A Poem" by Robert Frost:

The sentencing goes blithely on its way
  And takes the playfully objected rhyme
As surely as it keeps the stroke and time
  In having its undeviable say.

The raccoon's nose twitched as if black flies swarmed over the printed page. Did he smell the misspelled *undeniable*? (Clearly an editor oversight for I am rarely mistaken.) Just sensing the wrong word can drive a listener mad. So I felt buoyed up. By July, drained out. Like most students he could not grasp the meaning of a poem, its ambiguity, the way a crawfish is not a fish, inspired my Pavlovian plan.

Since raccoons show a taste for small aquatic creatures, I filled a water bucket with crawdads. Using his fingered forefeet, he savored each crustacean while I recited the tersely worded *Red Wheelbarrow*. Suddenly he scurried off, a black and gray blur. Perhaps for him the Williams title meant a blood-red barrow, the grave mound caused by a crushing wheel. He never returned, leaving behind a bucketful of lessons for me to digest.

Tara Moghadam

Masking The Scent

anything dead

the white bellies
of rotting bullheads
churning in the cattails

the skunk that met the tire
head-on
last week

pond scum
blackened carcass
of frog
thin spiral
of goose squat

anything i can
throw myself
back on

roll to right
squirm into spine
deep into muck
sucked into skin

those other dogs'
snouts cocked
to the wind

they think they
can smell
every place i've been

— Dakota County —

Jane Graham George

Swine Judging Dakota County Fair

Plaid-shirt farmboys with bale-strong
arms leaning on the metal corrals,
grandmas, other pigs and handlers,
all watch breathlessly as a small
teen-aged girl and her black, white-
belted pig stand waiting for the judge
who speaks as though he hails
from one of the finest salons
in Europe, literary, I mean,
as if awarding the Prix Goncourt,
enunciating each honeyed word.
"Folks, this young lady does not poke or prod,
is at one with her charming Hampshire hog.
4-H or not, this is equanimity."
Though she really does look like Athena,
it isn't quite like hitting a home run
or sinking a putt from an improbable distance
which is why, once the judge awards the blue ribbon,
there's no arm pumping, no prom-spinning in place.
Something about a hog does bring you right back to earth.

Roger Parish

What I Remember

I was always an island

I was up in my nest
lying back in the soft

proliferation of my dreams
watching the clouds evolve

I was sleeping harmlessly
at the bottom of the pond
father on shore
jabbing my chest with a pole
get up get up get up
until I emerged bright with venom
mom said eat eat eat
work work work said dad
until sweat was my nemesis
and food made me sick

I was walking away down my spine
on one side the sun shone
on a thunderstorm moving in
as lightning snaked across its face
on the other side an empty night
with a black moon canceling stars
and I couldn't choose either one
nor could I walk all the way

I was shuffling through my thirties
a silly bachelor uncle
forever giving up
and yet the game went on

I was driving through my shadow
no end in sight

I was arguing with the moon
in a ruined city on a mountaintop
under a downpour of angels

I was keeping pace on foot
with a shadow made of flies
the late sun shining
between the bones of my hand

— Dodge County —

Ann M. Schauer

Canada Geese

This beautiful forty degree weather
has the migrating birds confused into staying
on Silver Lake.

I've parked and walked to the grocery
to buy a loaf of bread and some time
for their critical chatter;
a thousand individual sermons.

I gaze at them and their fluttering
white wings around me as I bend
to feed from my hands.

The man in the red pickup truck is more popular
with his six pails of corn pellets.
He unloads them one by one
and paints a line the length of the parking lot.

He thinks he gets a congregation of repeating responses
honking unrequested thank yous
and amens.

But you know and I know
that had the man gone missing
they would carry on in their own church
even on this January day.

Charles Waterman

On Leaving a Poetry Reading at an Old Folks' Home

for John Rezmerski

Two follow us out to the automobile.
They gyrate like almost identical ghosts,
not quite disappearing into each other.

They gibber the same things they said inside:
about the college one of them went to,
which is where I taught recently, reminding me
over and over, as if I could forget.

The other keeps asking.
"Have you been through the town of Byron?"
I think I have been through Byron many times
in the last half hour;
but I can't remember what it looked like
seventy-five years ago. She can.

It's funny how they keep forgetting what they said to me,
and yet can't forget the college they went to
or the town they grew up in.

I wish I could stay, look deep into their eyes,
be permanent for them. They are blowing away.
I wonder if they remember any of our poems.

For about the fifth time, I shake their tiny hands and say goodbye.
          Back up carefully, John;
they're still behind us!

— Douglas County —

Frances Lyksett

Runestone Saga

(Kensington, 1362)

The rough-hewn stone was ready, and he knelt
To brush away the dust with calloused hand;
Not one in all the silent group but felt
The moment's import. In this empty land,
They knew, in time, their runestone would be found
And read by bearded Vikings, tall and straight
Of limb as they who stood and made no sound,
While one inscribed the story of their fate.

He measured with his eyes the rough gray stone;
And with his heart, the weary length of days
That they had come. How many moons had shone
Upon their campfires in the forest maze
Since they had known a harbor where the cries
Of welcome had been loud on every tongue,
Where men could rest beneath the bright home skies,
And all the long adventure could be sung!

No song, but stone, would speak for them; he took
The clumsy tool in awkward hands; and, when
He had engraved the year, he paused to look
Again upon those rugged uncouth men.
"8 Goths and 22 Norwegians came"—
Their saga lives upon a stone once bare.
In runic staves, he pressed their humble claim;
"Hail Mary, save from evil!" was his prayer.

John Minczeski

The Fight

It was like a ballet
that broke out of nowhere
at 3 a.m., a Country Kitchen
in Alexandria, Minnesota,
as chairs scooched back and tipped over.

There were no words
for what it meant:
language had broken down
into grunts and thuds;

life had given them fists,
hammy cheeks, coffee
and half a donut lying on a table
next to the waitress tray.
The night manager
simply stepped to the phone and dialed.

You would have thought they loved each other,
the way their faces looked,
they could have been related.
Everything so quiet,
even the police car
pulled up with its siren off

after the two guys got into cars
and drove away. Everyone knew
who it was and where they'd gone
to sleep it off, and they told the cops,
"they was waltzing."

— Faribault County —

Richard Carr

Breakfast

Mom hollers *Breakfast!*
from downstairs.
Her distant voice begins a dream,
a crow flight over corn,
swooping round the silo
and toward the house, all dark
except the kitchen.
Mom hollers *Breakfast!*
from the kitchen.
Cold nose and cheeks
but warm in bed, I lie awake.
Waiting in the barn, my 4-H cow
hollers low for breakfast.
Bare feet on cracked linoleum,
I holler back, a crow call,
and smelling bacon,
I swoop downstairs.

Meredith R. Cook

Midsummer Celebration

Each year we stood and waited in the street
Before the house to watch the Fourth explode
Red, purple, gold, and green above the trees
Between us and the fairgrounds to the north.

This year they aimed the fireworks too low.
We heard the "chuff" that signaled "going up"—

The "BANG." We saw a flash behind the trees
And little slicks of smoke like gray balloons

But not the swift chrysanthemum of light—
No scintillating rain of falling stars.

We walked as far north as the railroad tracks
Where we could see. Between the bursts of light
The yellow sparks of fireflies in the ditch
Flickered, and we danced to the mosquitoes.

Later, looking west along the tracks,
Seeing the white and red car lights on Main
Cross south, we knew it over; nonetheless,
We walked home backwards looking at the sky.

Mary Willette Hughes

A Taste for Reading

> *District 32 Country School*
> *Faribault County, Minnesota*
> *1938*

It is the first day of first grade, in the one-room
school house. Miss Agnes holds a shiny white
card showing a picture of clustered, ripe grapes.

I think about the smell of sun-warmed grapes,
about biting through the tough skin, sweet juice
flooding my mouth, and I hear the crunch
of slippery, oval seeds against my back teeth.

Teacher's eyes look straight at me.
She asks, *What color are the grapes?*

Purple, I say.

She points to the letters below the picture.
You said this word, Mary.

I purse my lips, whisper the word, and taste
purple on my tongue. With hungry eyes
I begin to own the world of words.

— Fillmore County —

Paul Walsh

Nature Lesson at Recess

Bright May embraces a sun-starved lawn.
Creatures of motion and noise, their prison doors loosed,
swarm the playground. Scholarly dispositions erased
by a thirty minute freedom, escapees from History, Spelling,
Arithmetic, and smell of chalk dust on an oily floor
charge the yard—a Bastille to be freed.

Arrested in progress by clamorous uproar, a creature of silent motion,
midway between sinkhole and weedy corner which in winter holds ice-
skating games, senses danger, and hoping to go unseen,
ceases its movement toward the lower ground.

But, the havenless, sliding symphony of silence has been eagled-out
by student eyes. Like jackals, they surround the glistening
unschooled creature. How reptilian mind scans
catalog of predators and storms—rainbow-like,
blossoms of spring-wear appear on every side!

Then, weather of confusion calms.
Professor Northhouse, master of erudition, descends
the anteroom steps, moves toward the gathered storm,

parts the painted mountains, dims the wave of screams,
and, prophet-like, sheds scales from eons of ignorance,
telling, in simple terms, how gophers, rats, mice,
and others of ill-repute are adder-seized, adder-devoured
by this friend of rural man.

All hear and, half-doubting, part the sea of school humanity,
allow spared prey a path to open ground—all but Joey,
who from woodpile, behind the school, and armed,
bolts into opened way precisely at the moment
brightly colored snake glides, unexpectedly, to freedom
in two writhing parts, one east, one west,
of a guillotine-sharp, double-edged ax
deep in cool Mother Earth.

— Freeborn County —

Marlys Tennyson Binger

Her Spirit Rides the Wind

High on a hill,
near a cobblestone
pump house, a sturdy
oak lends its strength
to mourners. The lake below
rolls, slapping
still shore, breaking
brittle silence. The sun
slips into October's
fiery dusk. A vital
minister delivers stern
Lutheran dogma to the family
over gaping crevice.
A space awaits next

to her husband and his
parents with only steps
down the slope to her first-born
daughter's premature resting
place. I, second-born daughter,
writhe, frozen in finality.

Steven Lewis Larson

Hornets are a Sign

Before the hornets moved into the front stairway siding, you could sit there and watch the sunset-lit mountains of charged water move across the Iowa and Minnesota border. Strobe lights flashed the little maple tree, Blackmer Avenue, water of Dane Bay, Lakeview School, and the great super cells themselves. Then I saw, sitting atop the tallest of all thunderheads, Jesus one hundred times his normal size, steering the storm with a gold-colored joy stick. This was the return promised by televangelists for decades and radio-evangelists before them. He was navigating those clouds right for the Freeborn County Fairgrounds. It reminded me of Santa arriving in downtown Truman with brown paper bags filled with peanuts, oranges, and hard candy (don't chew too hard on the rootbeer barrels, they'll crack your molar). This was way more important and exciting for those people who had confessed recently and hadn't had time to sin since. That was pretty much a handful of folks who were at the fairgrounds to take part in a horse show. Their average age was 78, pretty old to be hit by golden lightning bolts that coiled around them like bracelets on Cleopatra's arms. Jesus pulled them up to Himself and turned that storm toward Austin. Most Albert Leans were out of their houses by now, looking up at the most important event since the Shell Rock River was dammed to form Fountain Lake. There was a lot of confusion in the churches and most people started to smoke in bars and restaurants again. The next morning the hornets showed up and moved into the steps. I wanted to go out and look for storms, but I got bit on the inside of my right knee by one of those little bastards and it hurt like hell.

— Goodhue County —

Coleen L. Johnston

Farm Wedding

They paint the fence posts and tie them up in tulle,
    fit them with ferns and satin bows that shine in the morning sun.
        They build a bower of boxwood and giant hosta leaves
           where pearls peek out here and there like dew.
      Petunias—pink, purple and plum—they lay at the bride's feet,
        but hand her roses for her bouquet.
Windbreak rows of young caraganas and ash trees shade the aisle,
      neat rows of suits and fancy dresses on either side.
Every eye takes in the field of tall green corn
    lining the river valley like velvet
        just beyond where the groom stands shivering in his tux
          while the groomsmen sweat.
They see the new-mown meadow grass where
      white sandals and black oxfords make no sound.
    Swallows swoop above the guests,
        dipping low but never touching well-coiffed
hair or bald spots,
    as if someone is throwing rice before the rings have been exchanged.
All eyes watch the sky, where clouds gather,
    where infinity promises all that is imagined
        and what can never be.
            All souls are wed in wonder.

After dark, the cows will amble back
      into their pasture on the other side of the windbreak.
  They will turn their great blue-brown eyes to the tasseled corn
and smell the river.
      They will switch their tails as swallows touch their broad backs.
        and know their own infinity.
In the morning,
    gates will be opened. And closed.
    Bunks will be filled with ground feed,

waterers turned on.
Even then, the white fence posts will begin to weather,
their tulle having been carefully taken down and rolled on spools
to be used another day.
Once again the tractor will roll over the ground
where yesterday
the bride's satin slippers did not quite touch the earth.
A father will look down from the seat in his glass cabin
and see in the bent grass
the aisle of his cathedral—
in the play of swallows, the roof—
and in the silky corn
a promise of infinity
he vows to keep.

Beverly Voldseth

Highway 58 #300 2/1/2008

already the clock's tick pushes toward darkness
black cow statues in the cow yard
each silhouette a different posture
face toward pasture but caught still

already the calendar numbers fall off the page
weeds gather in clumps stubble sticks out of the snow
marks the tractor's path over summer field
reveals fall yields breadth and width of plow

I cannot choose but follow days behind
time passing in haphazard ways
engulfed in my own umbra that leans
toward sorrow and then toward praise

— Grant County —

James Elberling

Finding the Fragments

The old iron bridge spanning the creek rattled a bit as I
crossed over. I once tossed twigs upstream and ran to the
other side to see them float out. The twigs cut vee patterns
through the oil slicks from the bridge and rippled reflected
clouds in the flowing water.

I stopped at the crest of the hill.
The driveway should be here, no trace of it now.
Bean fields slope away on either side.
The little woods still stand, also the distant big woods.
The owner resisted the temptation to clear cut.

The house is in Ashby. Another room has been added.
The front porch is gone, replaced by a stoop.
A farmstead beyond the big woods claimed the barn,
now just a shed, so small in the shadow of blue steel bins.

The bean field ends in a stand of cattails bordering the creek.
On our walk to school my brothers and I crossed over
balanced on a board perched on two boulders. One spring,
flood water washed the plank away.
We had to go all the way to the bridge.

The school was a single room, eight grades, two outhouses
out back. The wood stove gave winter heat for the room
and warmed the hot lunch pot of baked beans or soup.

The building is now a museum in Elbow Lake,
much the same except the pump organ has been replaced
by a piano, and electric lights grace the ceiling.

You can still go home again to the country of your youth.

Streams still flow from the marshes into the lakes.
County roads still define the checkerboard of the land.
Just don't expect to find the pieces where you left them.

Angela Foster

Mother with Alzheimer's

She's a boat
tethered in choppy water
when the wind picks up
I'll rest my tired arms
drop my useless line
watch her drift
     alone
out to sea

— Hennepin County —

Ed-Bok Lee

Emergency

Slumped inside Hennepin County Emergency,
my eye wanders the wandering others,
each with no body to call a home at 3 AM—

Salvation shudders
blanketing hope to the music of CNN—

Sore-mouthed, wild eagle-eyed, prosthetic foot and shinplate
   airing itself;
a Black woman dripping red cornrows convenes

unconsciously with Jesus' mangled mullet—
The room, a marrow broth mid-December,
sweet and well beyond lust ....

Or is this soulless cinderblock building
the warm, artful heart of God? And our spirits
in fact billowing a dozen white curtains?

This is the mind burning itself naked ....
Meanwhile, the moon

recycles old love
through metallic ventricles;
casts shadows around

shrunken kidneys and livers ....
An infant, bundled in the tattooed, AIDS-gaunt arms

of a Native woman, mewls
a dilapidated tune; reaches up
at a soft-snoring Somali girl's sky blue head scarf—

Outside, a cloud lit
slowly wraps us in gauze.

Thien-bao Thuc Phi

light

At night,
when everything becomes debris
of light
and curving blackness,
slicing swathes into degrees
of darkness,

I understand that your love is my sundial:
the sun has dragged and the moon has draped 7 times

since last you kissed me,
and through those changes of brightness
I've crawled
to seek light in the arcing rims
and alcoves of your ears,
I'm hiding
in the delicious cave at the small of your back
the delight of its curves enough to sustain me.

I see you when the fluorescents keep giving out
on the subway car and the blinking blue lights
in the tunnels suddenly become everything,

the chinese man
at the canal street station, so close
to chinatown,
lines in his familiar face
holding more stories than
the hints of brightness
from the reluctant pockets
that feed his violin case.
He looks at me and we both understand
that no matter how many coins bury themselves
into his possession, he can never buy change.

And when I can't stand whispering
how much I love you into the darkness anymore,
I drive towards you, the lights in the eyes of my car
staring at stars,
the minus marks
on the highway subtracting the space between us.
I come to understand that at night
the absence of light
is your distance.
So when I kneel willingly before you
smelling of stardust,
my mouth starved
for your sunlight

I'll beg to feel with my fingers
the brightness caught in the blackness
of your hair

and I'll tell you that I need the light
radiating and rising from the horizon of your skin

and I'll tell you that I need the brightness
billowing from your breath

and I'll tell you that I need the delight
of your unspeakable perfection

and I'll tell you
that I need

I'll whisper this
begging for an ounce of brightness

the unique light
on the tips of your fingers
spirals inside of me

even when I close my eyes
you stain
the back of my eyelids orange

and I come to realize
eyes become light at the end of the tunnel
where I begin,

kisses become sundials,

hands become longitude and latitude
chasing the sun's shadow across time zones,

and fingertips become stars

your love becoming light

C. Mannheim

Light Rail in the Season of Giving

Her headscarf drawn tightly
      as much against the shame of exposure
      as against December's clipper wind
Her ungloved hand lightly runs
the length of the door (no longer automatic)
      now closed against the season's chill
She raises neither brow nor gaze
to those warmly seated within
but glides along the outside of the car

My eyes trace her uncertain progress:
      Thin, dark and lean, East African, I surmise
      her face, downturned, looks aged
      though younger, I'm sure, by several years than mine
I heft my overloaded backpack from my lap,
and scramble to my feet, springing several hurried steps
past passenger-filled seats to the train's rear door
where she stands outside lightly running her hand along the door
making no appeal

I press the blue dot, and when doors part to admit her
in heavily accented English I hear "Thank you"
as I head back toward my seat.
Turning and with gestures
I instruct her, "Push,"
my voice filled with sharpness
Sharp, because all the riders
seated round are 25 years younger
and able-bodied, except the overweight
youth in a motorized wheelchair
Too comfortable, perhaps,
with their cells and pods
or clutching at their Macy's Xmas bags
to offer a moment's simple help
to an old woman in need,
      cold, baffled, a long way from home,
      family and country, all likely demolished in war

At Cedar Station, she rises to leave,
but turns back to again bid thanks,
so grateful for a simple kindness
wrapped in sharpness
I gesture, while repeating the lesson: "Push!"
Sharp, I slowly see,
because she cannot fend for herself
because she is at the mercy of indifferent strangers
Because I, so easily, could be her.

Kay Foy

The Lutefisk Dinner at the Lebanon Lutheran Church

I watched the Lutheran ladies fume
When you wore your Halloween costume
To the Lebanon Lutefisk Dinner
With the straight-laced forgiven sinners.

You wore your buttonless St. Viney's
Mink coat, which looked like an old goat,
And your Gabby Hayes hat, which
You sewed jewelry on, like—"splat!"
You donned Bermuda shorts in winter,
Fringed to the hip, with a metallic gold shirt
And knee high moccasins.
You said you were a pirate.

We ate that rubber soaked in lye
And gave each other a high five.
We ate the pickled beets and the dead
Milk gravy poured over potato beds.
Then, we topped it off with rice pudding
And you brought your bag for looting.
Oh Lord, deliver us.

You thanked the cooks as we left the hall.
I didn't think to say thank you at all.

Your red hair matched the crisp cool air.
The moment was astoundingly rare,
And I heard some pigeons call in a fuss,
"Oh Lord, deliver us."

Ed-Bok Lee

Seasons of Hair

I know men who survive
by their women's hair, its scent
a force field each winter dawn
shuffling steps at the bus stop

In spring, smiles resurface, hands
hungry to unjam storm windows,
re-thread bolts and grease bicycle chains;
clanks under engine blocks
drive wasps crazy; a dancing
ankle turned on a wine bottle in the grass

Summer evenings around a picnic
table metropolis'd with food and condiments,
the man's fingers sweep the moon
from his wife's black mane, humming
of lovers in an oarless boat on the East Sea …
While breezes blanket our exhaustion
from an afternoon full of trees

But my favorite season is autumn,
when my father's evening tea changes color
for all the leaves fallen into the river,
and my mother rests on the sofa
after work and asks
me to remove any silver
from her hair
like sewing in reverse

Mike Rollin

16th Ave. Sketches: Today's lovers

> *"wells of magic"*
> — *Arthur Rimbaud*

In an Oldsmobile Custom Cruiser with simulated wood panels and a rusted sky-blue body, making out at the corner of 24th and 16th, a Latino couple—he with a shaved head, she with golden hoop earrings. Their muffler, if there still is a muffler, has quit for the day and forever. They kiss with the crazy loud engine running, the car inching forward as he leans further over to her in the passenger seat until one of them senses the small movement toward the oncoming traffic on 24th and he hits the brakes. They stop to laugh for a second—she pulls a wave of hair out of her eyes, he puts the car in park, and they go back to necking. They have no intention of crossing the intersection. The small cloud of blue exhaust from the Custom Cruiser does not reflect in the broken windshield glass beside them. Across the street it is shirts vs. skins on the court in Cockroach Park, and the rose-colored sandstone of la Iglesia Santo Rosario is still rose, because that is the color of those stones.

Thien-bao Thuc Phi

Waiting for a Cyclo in the Hood

26th Street, a one way,
flows by my house, keeps going right
out of the hood, before spilling into
Uptown: fertile delta of the young,
disturbingly hip, rich by no fault of their own,
nothing to do on a Saturday night but be beautiful.
I sit on the curb, far from lovely,
empty pocket's distance from rich,
wishing I knew
which way to go.
Back in Viet Nam I could

shout for a Cyclo, hold up a fist of small dong,
peel each dollar from the tension of my hand
and let them fly away to the Doppler Effect,
one by one,
scream the words to Prince's "1999" in two languages
and not once look behind me to see
if the cyclo driver was whispering:
this street is one way, I can't take you back
to where you came from, no matter how many American
dollar bills you give up
to the wind.

— Houston County —

Edith Thompson

Afterward

Close the door,
And draw the shutters too,
For he will look no more
Through the blue curtains of his eyes,
Nor will he come, all kind and wise,
To the locked doorway of these lips
To speak again, the comforting and wise.
      The house is empty.
      Gone who made it worth;
      The house is empty,
      Leave it to the earth.

Edith Thompson

Diminuendo

Flash! and the night splits open,
Crash! and its towers fall.
Silence and darkness follow
    Annihilating all,

All but the steady fiddling
Of a cricket's violin,
Quiet and reassuring
    After the monstrous din.

— Hubbard County —

Karen Herseth Wee

The Day the Ice Goes Out

We skirt the poplar forest
        to stare through mist
                out over the shape-shifting ice

Three days it takes   the glassy lake soon
        in a mostly watery guise—
                in constant response to wind

At the edge of its thinning   fat white ducks
        with black heads and backs and drab mates
                dive in   then pull

their pudgy sexy bodies up out of the water and onto the ice
        wings aflap   they happily bare their breasts
                to the biting wind

which harbors still its lingering cold wish to hold
the lake's dark damp face in thrall—
Spring—all is restless underneath

Sharon Harris

Life-Worn

the old dog
with several strokes behind her,
has lived more lives
than most cats.

she stands
at the corner
of her kennel
with aching joints.

her near-blind eyes
stare at the forest's edge.
she woofs quietly
at even intervals,

life-worn,
calling death,
asking the peaceful darkness
to come for her.

Michael Dennis Browne

Little Women

These little women have gray hair.
They wear print frocks and ankle socks.
Their hair is cropped.

Two days from Christmas, a mild snow.
As one by one I meet them,
Ruth tells me their names.
One kisses my hand.
One will not look at me.
One shudders and weeps on a couch.
One sways like a prize fighter,
rocking backwards and forwards on fixed feet,
throwing small punches.
One grinds her jaw around.
One sits smiling, as if at a wedding.
It is snowing, it is snowing.
Someone is being married in the snow.

For these gray girls I sing.
"A little child on the earth has been born."
It is a Flemish Carol,
which my father taught me.
"He came to earth but no home did He find."
The bare hall echoes like a bathroom,
I sing full-throated,
I feel like a bird among branches.
Do they hear? Do they hear the child's story?
I don't know how unraveled they are
behind those eyes,
I don't know if the doors
are closed or burning or whirling.
They seem like Ophelias who survived the stream.
Someone is being married.

Ruth circles with some of them. Dancing.
They shuffle and stamp. It is snowing.
"He came to the earth for the sake of us all.
He came to the earth for the sake of us all."
When later I ask Ruth
who, of all the minds at the institution,
are the most lost, she tells me
it is these.

LouAnn Shepard Muhm

Offering

> *"I shy away from transcendence."*
> *—Bill Borden*

We all do,
deer in the ditch.
white tails arcing
graceful as we flee
the passing numen,
leaping away
from bright lights
and broad wheels.

Or maybe we stay quiet,
heads down,
grazing,
ignoring that flash
that has passed us by
before.

Some will stand frozen,
make a wrong step,
then, nicked and limping,
bleed into the woods.

But sometimes there is one
who runs headlong
to the road,
sacrificing everything
to get behind
that glass.

David Wee

September Loon

Our loon appears again this morning
Every day he is here
Alone
As dozens more gather in the middle of the lake
He comes in close to us
Calm, quiet, blackandwhite, red eye,
Swimming north.

Will he fly south with the others?
Has he chosen his solitude
Or is he a rejected one,
Or injured, fated to die
When the ice comes?

Today a seagull comes to swim with him
While the other gulls squawk over minnows
And swoop away.

Odd couple!
What do they speak to each other
In loonlanguage and gulltalk?
If we knew,
We would be blessed …
Perhaps saved.

Lou Ann Shepard Muhm

Shoveling Out

You've stayed away from the windows
unwilling to look at the yard
full of unfinished chores
and death
and then, overnight,

the snow,
a foot or more
a gift, a day
maybe two if you're lucky,
of clean white forgetting
until the mailman leaves you a note,
a reminder
that beauty is treacherous.
It is not until
you get out in it
and dig
pain singing
in every muscle
that you realize
the terrible weight.

— Isanti County —

Charmaine Pappas Donovan

Bicycling Highway 65

Twice I two-wheeled it through Cambridge,
once above my own bicycle pedals,
another time on the back of a Santana tandem
bobbing to the time of piston legs in front of me.

Sometimes the only thing a tired bicyclist considers
is the sun's heat settling on asphalt and skin,
a dryness drawing attention to the phlegmy throat,
or panting that sounds like someone in hot pursuit

of you—only it is you—your chest heaving,
working its way into a breathing rhythm
until you squint, wishing the water tower closer
so you can stop, stretch, stand—ride on.

On to something else smaller growing larger,
as you pass pastures with numbered street signs,
wondering if cows ever receive mail along this road,
this suburb of a town you plan to soon wheel through.

— Itasca County —

Josephine Brower

Lines to Jacob Brower

Do not mourn if skies are drear,
I will give you a Torch to carry.
Your heart is young, brave pioneer,
The way—so difficult and long—
Well needs the toil
Strong hearts can bear.
Light each lake and stream and hollow—
The Torch, your guide—Itasca's fame,
Linked with glory and your name,
True finder of the river's source,
Now every man may follow.

Edward Reimer Brandt

The Minnesota Mississippi

The mighty Mississippi river flows
Where piney woods and platted cities grow
Up north. Its wish is its command. Heave ho!
Here, childlike, as it pleases, there it goes.

Where pebbles sleep, the infant current shows
No signs of vehemence. In bonny bow,
The mighty Mississippi river flows
Where piney woods and platted cities grow,

Itasca-born, the Baby Bunyan knows
No ordinary limits and no woe
Of weakness long. It wills; it wins. No foe
Can match it. Even when the blizzard blows,
The mighty Mississippi river flows
Where piney woods and platted cities grow.

Louis Jenkins

Mushroom Hunting

Here I am, as usual, wandering vaguely through a dark wood. Just
when I think I know something, when I think I have discerned some
pattern, a certain strategy—ah, they grow on the north edge of the
low mossy spots—I find one on top of a rise and it shoots my theory
all to hell. Every time I find one it's a surprise. The truth is there is
no thought that goes into this. These things just pop up. And all this
thinking, this human consciousness, isn't what it's cracked up to be.
Some inert matter somehow gets itself together, pokes itself up from
the ground, gets some ideas and goes walking around, wanting and
worrying, gets angry, takes a kick at the dog and falls apart.

Jeanne Showers Knoop

The Penalty

Man, you have wasted earth's substance
In sating your own desires,
You have gutted the hills of their treasure
In garnering coal for your fires,

You have swept through the forests like madmen,
Slashing and burning in greed,
Great tools have gone skimming earth's riches;
Stop, wastrel! Will you not heed?
God gave us earth and her bounty,
So faithlessly have you kept trust,
That earth in reprisal cries forfeit
And gathers your bones to her dust.

This poem was originally published in the 1958 Centennial issue of The Moccasin.

— Jackson County —

Karsten Piper

Speeding South

The shadow driving my truck's shadow at seventy,
seventy, seventy, is scuffed across the face
by golden ditch-grass, thumped
by pheasants and red-wings, lashed
by line after powerline, and beaten
once through its colorless head
by a ball cap, slat cross, and spray
of memorial flowers.

What skimming shadow at seventy, seventy
ever sees what hits it, ever knows
it never saw the sun?

— Kanabec County —

Robert E. Caldwell

Remember

Poised on a wind blown reed the lark is singing,
And springtime winds and lacy clouds are winging—
Blue mist is on the river—hills are green
Where cattle grazed beyond the willow's screen.
But, over there where hate has lately spoken,
The dove lies hurt, her once bright pinions broken;
A crimson light has swept a fertile land
And left the rose to wither in Death's hand.
Are not the songs of lark or bluebird singing
Far sweeter than the trumpet's war cry ringing?
Remember Flanders and the patterned rows
Of lonely crosses where the poppy blows!

Robert E. Caldwell

Submarine

Gray
Slithering
Serpent of the sea ...
Uprearing ugly head,
It hisses ... strikes ...

Then,
Vanishing
Beneath the writhing seas,
It leaves ... destruction ...
Death!

— Kandiyohi County —

John Calvin Rezmerski

Willmar at Night

I have been to Willmar, Minnesota,
where the houses look pious.
At night they hear noises,
metal wheels squeaking and hissing,
the throb of engines biding their time.
The houses turn over in their sleep,
dreaming of following boxcars,
windows wide open, wind whupping
through parlors and bedrooms,
finally, in Fargo or St. Paul,
letting strangers enter
with whiskey and loud stereos.
I have been to Willmar, slept in Willmar,
crossed the tracks in Willmar at night.

— Kittson County —

Margot Fortunato Galt

Quick Spring

1.
The ditches are flowing on Highway 11
along the border with Canada.
Mounds of snow erode to grit,
The sky lifts immense skirts

into the bowl of heaven. Slowly
the sun pushes its way north.

2.
Raymond has written a poem.
His class is gifted in poetry
but Raymond (absent the first day)
has put a white horse
    "String-tailed"
    "Galloping glory"
    "Winter sufferer"
    "Non-meat eater"
    "Hay chomper"
    "Baby maker"
    "Friendly creature"
on the page. He writes
    "You
     You
     You
     Come back soon."

3.
City-dweller, smart with words, I ask,
Did the horse bolt its traces?
It died, he says.
Raymond's teachers
can't quite believe that
Raymond the LD,
whose older brothers
quit school, who lost his
favorite brother to a farm
accident and hasn't
been the same since, Raymond
with no social graces
who can't read his own poem,
Raymond did what?
The best in the class, I hug
the paper to my breast.
Tell him, they insist, tell him.
Maybe he'll stay in school.

4.
For a moment, their faces radiant
they forget how hard it can be,
like the drying crust of winter
a sky rife with snow
a white horse, its outline
edging into oblivion—sway-
backed, head tossed yet
still sweet still visible
among a thousand
swirling words.

— Koochiching County —

Dennis Herschbach

Coldest of the Cold

It's thirty below in Frostbite Falls.
Rocky and Bullwinkle hunker down;
Boris and Natasha skulk about,
and the place is a frozen chunk of ice.

It's thirty below zero.
International Falls rejoices;
test cars sit on solid lakes,
batteries ever ready to fire up.

It's thirty below where Ojibway ruled,
their "neighbor lakes and rivers"
now gripped tight in silence
by nature's strangling, icy hand.

Koochiching, a native name,
cartoon home of agents and bumbling spies,
cold experiment capital of the world;
your rivers and lakes make good neighbors.

Louis Jenkins

A New Poem

I am driving again, the back roads of northern Minnesota, on my way from A to B, through the spruce and tamarack. To amuse myself I compose a poem. It is the same poem I wrote yesterday, the same poem I wrote last week, the same poem I always write, but it helps to pass the time. It's September and everything has gone to seed, the maple leaves are beginning to turn and the warblers are on their way south. The tansy and goldenrod in the ditches are covered with dust. Already my hair has turned gray. The dark comes much earlier now. Soon winter will come. I sigh and wonder, where has the time gone?

Matt Rasmussen

This Place

The hunters lie down
in a cold field,
their breath pluming

like a pod of whales.
A boat unzips the river
and on the bank,

the houses are pinned
to their long shadows.
Jabbed through the sky

the moon's fingertip is
blindly accusing everyone.
The paper mill's

slender nozzles glug
tan clouds, stirred quickly
into the towering wind.

Dawn falls off, but something
has been nailed to the air
telling us we're wrong.

Our lives turn their noses
into the breeze and bolt.
Spiraling down barreled eyes

into the flinching chamber
of the mind we find: the heart's
simple meat can be cut open,

but no love will spill.
A boy sprints through birches,
enters a clearing, becomes a deer.

— Lac qui Parle —

Rebecca Taylor Fremo

Lac qui Parle Show and Tell

He crosses the bridge and studies its bolts,
tests iron welded firm and strong.
Last used 1876, he notes, a good year for bridges.
I find nests tucked in its aging ridges
and wonder: Was it a good one for the birds?
We spend most Sundays touring our lives.
Today an aging lakeside county park,
its bridge now merely scenery,
needs us to write its history.
It's my turn now for show and tell.

We frame things differently at the park:
He sees abandoned public land;

I feel my need for stillness soothed,
And yet, we know we both are moved
by every place that speaks to us.

Last Sunday in his western town
frigid air blew straight from Norway,
stinging my cheeks and chilling my bones
while we wandered out among the stones
reading stories where his family lies.

We drove fast past his father's farm,
our horizon lost in the pick-up's dust.
I squinted at an open field to see the boy he must have been;
he counted posts and skirted gates that tried for years to fence him in.
His grown man's hands just clenched that wheel.

I envy him his home, his dead, the stillness
of his prairie town. Endless acres to show;
plenty of time to tell. Late at night the cups all rose
to combine survivors and cornpicker heroes.
All drink to what is right and true and rooted

in the fertile ground. I toast our Sunday show
and tell, hoping words will mark my life.
Lasting words—if I might stay.
And then I think, I should pray.
I am witnessing miracles here.

— Lake County —

Jean L. Childers

Ode to Section Thirty School

Fresh, blue, alcohol fragrance
filled the hall.
It was newsletter day.
Mrs. S. would let us hand-crank it
if we were excruciatingly good.

The cartons of milk held a wax taste
for those first few cold sips.
Crisp sweet graham cracker squares
made snacktime a treat.

In the basement we'd shiver and chatter
between stone walls, lined up at lunch tables.

Later, we'd listen to each other's settling-in whispers
as we all lay down on our braided rugs brought from home
for the afternoon's nap.
Shhhh, all quiet, children.

A prairie-grass field took over
after they tore the schoolhouse down.
Kids bused to town.
Gone are the seventeen steps up,
the swings,
the two classrooms, the gym,
the hall with the mimeograph machine.

Ruth Wahlberg

When Grandpa Took Me Walking Through the Town

(Two Harbors, Minnesota)

When Grandpa took me walking through the town
And tipped his hat to ladies, young and old,
Shook hands with all the menfolk on our way,
I mused, with childlike curiosity,
"He must know every person on the street!"
When Grandpa took me walking through the town,
The corner drug store was a favorite stop.
One dollar bought his reading glasses there;
He paid a nickel for my ice cream cone.
Sometimes we went into the butcher shop
And shuffled through the sawdust on the floor.
There I would get a juicy pickle, free.
It thrilled us when we saw a brand new car,
All shiny black; the wheels had wooden spokes.
He tipped his hat to ladies, young and old,
When Grandpa took me walking through the town.

— Lake of the Woods County —

Inez Jane Dopp

First Frost

The penetrating perfume
Lumps in my throat and locks
In scent of long-gone childhood
And my mother's four o'clocks.

For years I dared not plant them,
Homesickness held its clutch;

At last, nostalgia softened—
Fragrance relaxed its touch.

The black night before the freeze-up—
Frost fairies stretching their fingers,
I stand by the four-o'clock flowers
In tears; but sweetness lingers

Through the snowbound months of winter,
And remembrance fills soul's needs.
I think of my four-o'clock mother,
Then in spring I plant the seeds.

— Le Sueur County —

Cary Waterman

First Thaw

> *for Bridgit*

By noon winter is already dead
and the fog drapes LeSueur County
like a congregation of ghosts.
They hold hands around the tree trunks,
and in the folds of their winding sheets
they hide what my eyes need to see.

We lose our balance in this weather.
We squint to tell the earth from the air
and reach for familiar things—
a tree or the smell of an animal to steady us.

All day my daughter said there were voices singing.
They made her feel possessed.

Like the voices of the womb
they danced against each other singing
Come—
Spring runs off the hills like a mad woman.
Don't wait!

Alixa Doom

Coyote

There are late winter reports of coyote
wailing across the river.
Neighbors skating at night under the stars
hear the cry that does not belong
to anything inside their lives.

The city crawls out across the country,
raw buildings squat at the edge of the woods
like extraterrestrial tourists,
and the coyote moves in closer.
I want to hear it too. I walk out again and again
tracking coyote sound
down the foothills
of another life.

Coyotes have crossed the river!
I follow the soft trail back
through clouds of plum blossom,
bunches of Sweet Williams,
watch for the light blur of coyote,
a flurring movement
drifting sideways through cedar,
a mere ripple of fur.

Coyote travels the earth
as if its heart
carries no weight at all.

— Lincoln County —

Jorie Miller

Illegitimate Child

This was when I could understand without understanding anything. I didn't ask *Where is Daddy?* or *Who is that man*? or *Why are we moving*? When did the questions start? I know the place the story begins. I give you a sandbox made from a tractor tire. I give you a metal ring in a cement cistern cover. You want circles? I give you the plate that covered the hole in the wall where the stovepipe used to be. Round also was the enamel basin we washed dishes in, the yellow yolk of the egg. My grandfather dipped the tip of his toast, bread sliced diagonally and buttered. And the black dog, my dog, named Pabst, ran as fast as he could around the white house with the blue roof encouraged by my grandmother swinging her arms to make him go. Cherry pie, apple pie, pumpkin pie round. Canning lid round. The hollyhock buds were round and the bright moon shining over the dried corn. The winter wind blew from one end of Lincoln County, from the edge of South Dakota, straight on to the Mississippi. I didn't know to ask *When will the wind stop*? I didn't ask. I stood on top of the round hassock. I turned the hassock on its side and walked its curve, rolling from one end of the living room to the other, turned and did it again.

Joe Paddock

Waiting for Spring

Out-talking geese,
but making less sense,
we migrate constantly
to winter.

That springtime of nights:
goose-babble moonlight blend
over prairie,
the flocks riding
thousands of miles of wind
as ice drifts north.

Walking alone on moonlit prairie,
goose talk falling through the night
like spring snow:
       ankle deep in goose joy
       I'm filled with love,
       but can't fly.

Ah, the geese,
at home in the wind,
the marshes, the seasons.

Who am I? Who are we?
What are we to do?

— Lyon County —

Philip Dacey

The Day's Menu

Marshall, Minnesota

The time I told my daughter her Aunt Joan,
at fifty-one, had most likely died a virgin,
we'd stopped mid-afternoon for coffee at Perkins—
I don't know how the subject came up; Fay
and I just talked a lot about a lot—
all the other customers, it seemed, couples

long retired off their Minnesota farms,
now killing a time of day they'd always spent
hard at work alone, him outside, her inside,
and practicing their usual discipline
of silence over pie she could outdo,
or even blindness in the face of partners,
as if the decades, some all-too efficient
waitress, had wiped them both invisible.

So when my teenaged daughter, for quite a while
by then herself a practicing non-virgin,
learned the truth, it so shocked her, or maybe
shamed her, to think a relative of hers
could have lived, or, rather, not lived such a life,
that she forgot completely where she was
and, eyes widening in wild surmise as on
some peak of disbelief in Lyon County,
exclaimed in rising tones, "Aunt Joan died a virgin?!?"

Her voice carried like an order to the cook,
and you could hear utensils dropping all over Perkins,
onto pie plates, coffee saucers, tabletops,
intakes of breath, talk sotto voce, or not
so sotto: "Charlie, did you hear what I heard?"
Fay's words had replaced the special of the day.
Spouses spoke to each other for the first time
the whole pie-slice long, and Fay and I became
the object of stares across the rims of cups.

"Not certain but likely," I said. "A few years in
the convent. Afterwards, she dated again,
said she wanted to marry someday, and she
was beautiful—her pictures don't lie—but nothing
even a little lasting developed. I believe
the Catholic Church had done a number on her,
and she was saving herself for the marriage bed,
the holy sacrament, but no man was buying."

I remember Fay shivering a kind of stage shiver,
as when someone in a movie mentions the monster
roaming loose, or maybe not so stage at all:

she'd seen a real monster, or at least heard of it,
the worst kind, monster of absence, missed chances,
and felt its breath blowing down her pagan neck.
Her coffee was black and strong, and she took a long sip.

In my weaker moments, I like to think Fay's words
were less the daily special than appetizers,
spurs to hunger, and that one or two couples
looked up into eyes not lately noticed
and now seeming fresh, new, virginal,
behind which flashed the thought of losing what
they'd lost before, and would love to lose again.

David Pichaske

The Grandfathers

(after reading Giants in the Earth)

Gudmundson, Olson, Peturson, Josephson,
Williamson, Anderson, Olafson, Hallgrimson.

In these graves sleep the founders of the kingdom,
below arching elms, their branches bowed
like the vaults of Trondheim Cathedral.

Hanson, Benson, Sigurdson, Peterson,
Björnson, Rafnson, Jonason, Henrickson.

In the cycles of seasons their lives unwound,
in fields of ripening wheat and hay,
in the white wilderness of prairie winter.

Nicholson, Erickson, Högnason, Johnson,
Thordarson, Thorsteinson, Magnuson, Guttormsson.

Out on the edge of distant South Dakota
the sun sets behind the grave of Johann Kristjan Johannson.
He dreams dreams unbroken as the snow-covered prairie.

Margaret Hasse

Norwegian Grandmother's Song

Little yellow canary, sing to me, sing.
Sing to me of Bergen where cold seas
shook their sheets.
The rocking ship made me empty
my stomach into a pail over and again.
By water I came to this country,
by train I went to its prairie.
Oh, my husband was a beautiful boy
a Swede who learned
to lay bricks for our living.
He was a tall tower to my tiny frame.
I clung to him like a vine
of bush beans on a stake.
Girls we had, boys we had
with names that turned back
to tell where we were born:
Ingrid and Kristin, Fredrik and Lars.
The Red River ran behind the house
where giant cottonwood trees
clustered at the banks
like thirsty animals.
Little yellow canary,
from your cage in my kitchen,
sing to me, sing.

Florence Dacey

Prairie Weather

Winter storms are fierce, pulling us away from meager mind.
Snow catapults under our doors and corrals cars into single lanes.
Wind sprouts white talons. It throws up partitions
between us and the landmarks we live by.

Blizzards pull us down into fitful isolation.
We peer befuddled out of small islands
we have breathed onto frosty windowpanes.
When it clears a bit, we hurry to town for bread and milk.

In early summer the air grows heavy
and pulses like an artery ready to burst.
Ahead of one tornado, tufted layers of grey cloud
scout silently, going too fast and packed to the limit.

The twister roars over that hill, down into the river valley.
One old man dies, under his pick-up.
Broken-off trees by the road keep the history
fresh in our album of fears.

In between, rare floods sometimes accompany spring blizzards.
Old and young fill sandbags together. The talk is easy, the topic set.
The river has its way a while, gives misery a muddy suit,
takes back some land we thought we owned.

When the great storms begin,
I stand in my backyard prairie circle garden.
I gauge and, if I must, call for some mercy.
But usually I call in silence and inward exhilaration for the storm.

In guilt and horror at human folly,
in rage and in wonder at all our power,
I call and call to be confounded
by such weather.

Philip Dacey

The Regular

Bagels and Brew, Marshall, Minnesota

Grandpa McGinn made a home at the corner bar.
He'd enter, nod, and the drink appeared, a Bud.
I've always wanted to be a regular.

To be at home away from home, not far
but just enough. There, in dim light, freedom stood,
a bottle like a name, McGinn, on the polished bar.

He'd lost his first home, Ireland. Mary Moore
made a second for him in the neighborhood
where Nolan's, a third, counted him a regular.

So his ghost was whispering in my ear when the door
of Bagels and Brew first opened: I knew I had
to make a home at my local coffee bar,

to enter, nod, and watch the owner pour
a dark roast blend, my choice, without a word.
And I succeeded. I'm now a regular.

To be known. Even in miniature.
Family, without the knives of blood.
I enter to be saved, nod like one at prayer,

the light as dim as in the home of God.
Grandpa McGinn made a church of the corner bar.
My communion's black, no sugar, and regular.

— Mahnomen County —

Marcie R. Rendon

grandmother walks

> grandmother walks moonlit trails
> sucking maple syrup cubes
> birchbark wraps itself around her
> while black bear guards her path

at the water's edge,
in a rock upon the path
flickering in an evening flame
i see her face

— Marshall County —

John Calvin Rezmerski

Momentum

for Mike Doman

Tearing along somewhere near Grygla,
he delights in taking a curve
almost as a swerve,
out into a fast straightaway.
In a moment, up from the ditch,
a gray blur not a dog
dashes almost in front of his car,
but stays on the shoulder.

Glancing over its shoulder
at his braking to match its speed,
the wolf speeds up to pace him.
They are side by side, eye to eye,
bonded by tense momentum
for three moments or so—
until it swerves back into the ditch,
leaving him to drive straight ahead
into his empty rear-view mirror,
now past any point where
stopping could reveal anything more.
The wolf exits his life
as he departs the wolf's,
the two of them abandoning curiosity,
alike for four moments or so,
then different as ever before.

— **Martin County** —

Stash Hempeck

Death of a CowBoy

You are ten and I am twelve
that spring Sunday afternoon
we spend an hour in your haymow
moving all those green and gold and brown
bales into piles, building hills
and valleys full of trees and tunnels,
towers of stones,
snakes and scorpions.

As I am your guest,
you give me your favorite pistol
to use, because its black and silver metal
always has the most power.

But your kindness does me no good.
At first I think you are besting me
because you are younger
and faster
and a better shot.
But just before your last bullet
takes me in the center of my chest,
I realize

I have already died.

Bonnie Ann Wolle

Legacy of Interlachen Park

The Fairmont Sentinel:
"Interlaken Park
is the most beautiful and best equipped amusement
park in the Northwest and Fairmont's
biggest asset." 1917

For several years it drew crowds—on weekends,
4,000 or more. People came for miles.
Children would be charmed
by the seals, deer, parrot, bears, lion,
monkeys, an ape (that escaped!), ostriches
that loved to graze on dandelions—and more!
One could watch a baseball game at the diamond,
bring a swimming suit and experience
the thrill of the water toboggan slide,
splashing into the waiting lake
with shrieks of delight.
Care to join in on the 4th of July festivities?
Mill among 20,000 visitors for a day of picnicking,
horse races at the hippodrome and perhaps
some auto polo. Or stroll through the finely groomed
Japanese Gardens, inhaling the sensations
of bursting blooms along immaculate grounds

complete with gracefully designed islands between
Hall and Amber Lake.
Don't miss William Jennings Bryan pour out heartfelt
patriotism from the bandstand in the amphitheater—
or the Indian Pageant held at nightfall with canoes
gliding silently across Amber Lake,
spurred on by insistent drumbeats and culminating
with flaming arrows arcing across the summer sky.
Or spend a night out at the Inn—sitting so stately atop the grassy
knoll above the beach—and dine off a menu
likened to that of California cuisine (for just $1.00) followed
by dancing to the Interlaken Waltz at the pavilion.
If the Million Dollar Orchestra plays, there're likely
to be 10,000 fans! The soda fountain will be busy!
Something to please everyone—
cones dripping with ice cream and memories!

— McLeod County —

John Calvin Rezmerski

Practical Lessons: Staying Cool

A guy in Glencoe says to me that
way back when he was fourteen
and helping with the harvest
him and his highschool buddies
who was helping harvest too
would go right along with the regular hands
after quitting time
to some joint in Stewart or Brownton
and they could get a tall cool one
no questions asked or nothing
as long as they looked scruffy enough
like they done a fair day's work
and as long as they could reach up
and slap their dime on the bar

and didn't talk smart to the owner
or seem too eager or get too fancy.

Like the time he got eighty-sixed
for asking for a Budweiser
instead of the local brew
that was supposed to be good enough
for the likes of a small fry like him.
All through the next two weeks
he had to get another kid
to get a short glass of beer for him
and take it around back
where nobody was likely to
see him drink even a boy's
version of a man's drink.

And he says nobody never said
a word that sounded like
they felt a bit sorry for him.

Ann Reid

(a victim of stroke)

The Fog

The fog returns
Misting the eye
Softening the corners of the mind
Chilling the cheek with its weight
Touching the tongue with cloying lull
Clinging to the arm and leg
Creating slow-motion
Curling into the being
Numbing   freezing   stupifying
Frustrating the senses
Making goals seem
Almost unreachable   almost
The fog returns   the fog

— Meeker County —

Joe Paddock

Kingsryder and McGraw

There were Kingsryder and McGraw
back then. McGraw ran the coffee shop,
and Kingsryder was an old man
who dressed each day in a black suit
and black, high-topped old man's shoes,
and carried a cane for the power that was in it.

> Back then
> it seemed that all of this had gone on forever,
> but these prairies had only just been turned.
> This was our first generation of old men,
> violent as old bull buffalo on their knees, bubbling
> their last blood.

Each day at three in the afternoon, Kingsryder,
entering the coffee shop, all bustle and self-importance
around some emptiness within, I suppose,
> or maybe just that storm
> of hellish fun,
would whack his cane on the counter
for attention,
call for donuts and coffee,
begin his noisy complaint, dead pan:
"McGraw, you got an old garbage pile 'round back
where you get these donuts?"
Then lifts his cup: "McGraw,
whose radiator'd you drain today?"

> These two men over many years
> had never once embraced.
> Never once thrown a friendly arm around
> the other's shoulder.
> Perhaps, even, never once shaken hands.

And McGraw, over the years, always irritated,
would only say, "Kingsryder, one of these days
I'm gonna shoot you!"
And *whack!* goes the cane across a counter that
not twenty years back had been an oak
on the Darwin Prairie.

"Draw your weapon, McGraw! Play your hand!"

And so McGraw sent away somewhere
for a box of blanks
for his old hog-leg revolver,
and comes the day—there's a half-dozen coffee soaks
there—when Kingsryder asks:
"McGraw, you got a deal with old Moon Beckstrand
what cleans the streets?"
And McGraw says deadly between his teeth:
"Kingsryder, I've told you!"
Then he reaches slow under the counter,
comes up with his revolver,
and the place is so still
that you can hear
a crow cawing for something lost
way off at the edge of town.
Kingsryder's cane wavers. Not a snake-tongue flicker,
but a waver, like the antenna
of a confused insect.

How does an old Indian fighter die,
when, in fact, he'd never really…?

McGraw's face is cold.
KA-BAM! goes the piece.
Kingsryder's eyes show white in a faint,
and he slides from his stool to the floor,
and the six coffee drinkers pass through the door
like whippets, shouting:

"MCGRAW SHOT KINGSRYDER!
MCGRAW SHOT KINGSRYDER!"
We laughed about it for years. It tuned up our lives,

and emptied Kingsryder of half his style.
Who's to say the fright didn't knock a bit
from the tail end of Kingsryder's days?
Or who's to say Kingsryder's insults hadn't done
as much for McGraw?

They're both gone now.
They were our first generation of old men,
violent as old bull buffalo on their knees, bubbling
their last blood.

Barbara Enright

The Ladies of the Northern Prairie

Patchwork people, homespun in a threadbare culture,
Woven together in heritage
And in their welcome bondage to the earth under their nails.

Women's circle meetings—roundly searching the Scripture—
Church work and gossip weaving the quilt of their lives.
Hearty, strong and thrifty women, knowing depth
            but afraid of abandonment and joy.

Thick wool and denim, stiff with hardness of their crust,
Encircling softness and the Belgian lace of their souls.
There is no time for delicacy
                        on the prairie.

The cold comes too swiftly, and the loneliness is a curse.
The men work, and take them, and their lacey soft insides—
And leave them the money, and the land,
                        and the cold.

And under the goose-down quilt, they shiver
And pray for more for their daughters
Than the earth
                        and the cold.

— Mille Lacs County —

Doris Bergstrom

At the Swanson Farm, 1930

After we have eaten and stacked the dishes,
cows milked and cream cans stored
in the cold water tank, we stroll down
the graveled hill to the crossroad,
turn our faces to the lowering sun.

Following the edge of swamp-land
we step into a pool of cool air.
Gramma cautions we are walking into ghosts,
their restless forms rousing to haunt the night
gathering in moon-shaded hollows, hovering
over the plum orchard, resting on cupolas
of the barn roof, and we must carefully,
respectfully pass through them.
At our backs the veil closes, the air warms
and our feet crunch on.

We kids hang over the concrete bridge shading
the unnamed creek—its clear, lazy water
creeping beneath us, where long ago
plains bison wallowed at this water hole,
stepped their hooves into peat soil,
the peat sinking them, holding them,
their bleached bones uncovered by road crew
widening the ditch that, regular as springtime,
flooded from winter snow.

Had Gramma known then of bison bones
she likely would have told us we were stepping
into the snorting breaths of these beasts

and my sister and I would ponder this
falling asleep on antique couches
in the long porch
dreaming of a pounding herd
rushing to drink this wild brew.

— Morrison County —

Laura L. Hansen

Last Train Song

I'm starting to get up at night
just to listen to their songs.
I stand in the bare moonlight
letting their aah-aah-oooo
wash over me like gentle rain.
The songs come out of the south,
as soft woo-wooing wavering
in the distance, eerie as silence,
aah-aah oooo, whoo-a-whoo,
growing louder, nearer,
then passing on. Already
I miss their yodeling,
each engineer playing
a distinctive song, each song
a shimmer across the water.
Soon the trains will be silent,
their nighttime revelries
banned in our town,
and soon only a few of us
will awake restless and troubled,
unable to bear the long quiet.

Margaret Hasse

Winter Blessing

Snow saddles the palomino ponies
which the cold jockey
of winter rides.
One dowdy old mare
wears an uncurried undercoat.
She nudges broken bales of hay,
chews placidly, her teeth
pegged like piano keys.

When I enter the paddock
as a woman dissolving
into the grey landscape
of middle age,
she lifts her long face to show
the coal of curiosity
and the white crescents
of doubt in her eyes.

From a grave stillness,
her whole body startles.
Rotating on a back hoof,
she aims toward the open gate.
She bucks, blasts gas
and flashes the willow switch
of her tail reminding me
of the spunk a girl takes
to grow old.

—Mower County—

Chris York

The Bonfire

1.

It seemed like hours;
we drank our beer.
No one said a word.

I was thinking of the banjo
and its giddy melancholy.

2.

And I was thinking
of the fire late at night,
how it was like home:
still warm and vibrant
at its heart, but creeping
inward—

and how, when we were young,
we skulked away—in pairs
to the dark corners of barns
or alone down blustery highways
that opened up to anywhere.

Radiant embers buoyed
by the updraft. Many caught
no current and fell and settled;
burnt ash on the fringe.
Here, in Blooming Prairie,
at the farm.

3.

I was thinking that Monday the smell
of smoke will linger in my jacket;
bitter, pungent, opaque.

4.

I was thinking:
The stars are far away
(something so easy to learn,
but so hard to know).

— **Murray County** —

Janet Timmerman

At the County Fair

It is still a treat
to get free ice water
from the Culligan man
in small pointy cups.
The boys still take two
and tuck them up under
their T-shirts
parading in feminine guise,
like my brother did before the girls
smashed them to his chest with such
indignation that
he still wears the scar.

Janet Timmerman

MotherWill

There are few things harder than Buffalo Ridge rock,
and one of them is the will of my mother.
Age eighty-seven, she stands by the kitchen sink,
empty cereal bowl in her hand, and swears,
"That doctor can go to hell. No one's cutting off my tit.
That little lump doesn't bother me and I'm not going anywhere but to
    my chair for a nap!"
End of discussion;
and maybe her life.

She is 13 hands high, bent as an iron horseshoe
from years of bending
over in the garden,
over the washtub,
over a cake in the oven
checking its springy doneness with a poke of her fingertip.
This morning, when she draws herself up to an indignant height,
she seems very small and transparent.

Though I give every reason for seeing the doctor tomorrow,
she hears nothing and turns to clean up her breakfast dish.
I know I will go to see the oncologist alone
and listen to what my mother refuses to hear.
When I come home to tell her the options
she will consider only one.

Karsten Piper

The Word *flat*

The word *flat* is not—
not with its tower,
lookout,
and façade.

The *prairie*, though, stays low
for cursive miles before and after amber sun,
airy spaces dotted by a banking throng of starlings,
dotted by a single insect blown against a bending clover.

When you have visited,
don't note
how *flat*.

— Nicollet County —

Rebecca Taylor Fremo

Jesus Goes to the Dentist

This morning Jesus went to the dentist.
I know because I saw his car
parked right next to the hygienist's pick-up.
Vernon Center Meat Market, it reads,
her truck's siren call
to patients who aren't there for root canals,
but need a little routine maintenance
and might enjoy a good steak
afterwards.

I know the car belonged to Him
because it said so.
His name emblazoned the side.
I say "emblazoned" because
the car—American—
bore His name in all black letters
followed by a period.
(When black letters declare
the Savior's name to the world,
then punctuate themselves so finally,

the verb "emblazoned"
seems somehow
appropriate.)

The banana bright car
matched the banana bright sign
by the modest bricky church where he must live.
I see it from my own blue house, also modest.
A billboard points them to our town.
His pilgrims, I mean.
Jesus wants us all to know He lives
here, since He's unlisted.
An oversight, perhaps, or
His attempt to fool telemarketers.
Smart cookie, that Jesus.

So when I saw His car today,
top down in the dentist's lot,
I steered my Huffy off the path
(a beaten path—He'd want me to leave).
I detoured through the parking lot
then pedaled right close to His car,
hoping for a look inside.

Philip S. Bryant

A Little Spanish Speaking Island

The other day on the south end of town a group of young Latinos
barreled up in a bright red extended cab Ford pickup truck, with a
Dallas Cowboy star logo stuck on the left rear bumper and Texas
license plates. They all got out of the rear extended cab, yawned and
stretched their legs, smiling and all speaking rapidly in Spanish.
And suddenly the cold Minnesota March wind blew just a little bit
warmer and the sun got brighter and in the air were the smell of fresh
made tortillas and dark Michilitos poured in tall frosted glasses,
refried beans, pears, oranges, guitars, brass marching bands and
illuminated paintings and statues of Our Lady of Guadalupe and

strings of multicolored lights forming big wide toothy grins across these dark drab buildings and streets. And in the dirty crusted and melting snow I suddenly felt so warm and tropical—and smiled at one of the young boys who glared at first, but then smiled and nodded back to me, now on our little Spanish speaking island off the coast of Mazatlan, yet surrounded by cold northern ice and snow as well as the rest of these small town people standing around us who also heard these warm lovely musical sounds but couldn't feel the warmth that traveled all this way north and couldn't seem to thaw their icy frowns.

Alixa Doom

The Trees of St. Peter

After the Tornado, March 29, 1998

They stood so still among us
we didn't notice death languishing in leaves,
blurred as the squirrel's run along a limb.
Always there were the trees loitering over rooftops,
brooding in photos of young grandparents.
Swallowing the sounds of our daily lives,
they took us softly, even into darkness.

The day after the tornado, massive shafts
of trees splayed to the ground, every yard
black earth ripped by the roots
tangled like tentacles of great sea creatures.
Chain saws throttled the streets until
the entire length of each tree was chopped
and stacked for the caravan of trucks
that carried them to a burn pile east of town.
I squeezed my eyes against the death
of the trees, as if I could be blinded
by all their light leaving, and I wondered
how long a tree soul lingers.

Now an April sun enters the town like a blow.
Without trees we see the town's climb

to the top of the hill it is built on,
through shattered walls and door-less rooms
of buckled houses, the raw data of our lives
bewildered by the rain and the wind.

The air around us is immense
with ghostly oak and maple trees
and a wind that winnows their absence.

— Nobles County —

Chet Corey

We Travel Both Ways Now

I ask you to take the steering wheel.
We are driving north toward Marshall
at a blurred hour when any mailbox
along this road could be mistaken
for a young man walking into town.
I hold the cup from the thermos
and drive with my elbows—the way
my father drove home from Al's Bar
with the neon blaze of a cigarette
in his hazel eyes. His lips mumbled
in the way my mother's moved
over decades of glass rosary beads
in the stuffed, living room armchair.
You remind me about blind railroad
crossings and the speed limit signs.
We will drive south in the bluish dark
perhaps again as silent as we drove
after tonight's first half hour's talk.
I will not mention the stooped, old man
nor how the static on that café's radio

made me remember late summer storms.
There will be faces of barns in yardlight
and those islands of cloud on Lake Shetek
we only see when driving the hills south.
I will think of that town's man relieving
himself along a side street going home,
and I will bless the broken, white lines
on this road that carries our freight.
I cannot explain such things at all.

— Norman County —

Marcie R. Rendon

The Red River

A river
Gulps mud
Persistent rush
Roots bared
Asphalt and concrete
No match for nature's cleansing
Springtime water eats the banks
Spits it out to feed the Hudson Bay

Willow arms caress
Summer muddy water
Catfish lurk
Bullheads scour
Mosquito buzz
A covert cover
For cottonwoods to gossip
Up and down the river

Leaves drop
Until the trees are bare enough
For red-tinged water to catch
The harvest moon
The river feeds on perfect light
While fish and other water creatures
Dance through silted clay
Down, down on the riverbed

Solid hoofs on snowy hills
Grasp for purchase
Finally, at river's edge
At water holes drilled
Into two-feet thick ice
Cattle drink
The moisture of their labored breath
Mingles with the water flowing slowly north

— Olmsted County —

Yuko Taniguchi

Blue Eyes

I used to believe that people with blue
eyes saw everything in blue.
In summer, I longed to see

in blue like living underwater.
I dropped my eyes into a blue bottle
and asked my husband to carry it around.

Every day, he worked at the hospital; all the buildings
seemed colder. When his eyes peeped in the bottle,
I saw the well of tears moving behind his eyes.

When I woke up, it was already autumn.
All day, I gazed at my husband, busy
collecting red and yellow leaves in our yard.

Yuko Taniguchi

Foreign Wife Elegy

My language has its own world
where he doesn't know how to live,
but he should learn my language;
then he can call my mother to say
that I am dead. I drive too fast
and someone else drives too fast
and we crash on the icy road.
The death sweeps me away.
He can tell this to my mother
if he learns my language.
Her large yellow voice travels
and hits his body, but at least she knows
that I am dead, and if I die,
I want him to tell my mother
with his deep voice shaking.

Yuko Taniguchi

Ice Fishing

On the frozen lake, Dad makes a hole with a large silver
stick. We stand on the bright snow. I could squeeze

my body through this hole like a snake. I want to
see the other side of the closed earth, but the water would

sting my body with its sharp needles. I was not made
to see every side of the earth. I hook a small fish

attached to a clear line, to a rod, and to my hand;
we control everything here.

Dad says a fish's mouth does not feel pain when it
swallows the hook. He says this because I am only
six years old. I prepare a guest room for the fish:
a blue bucket from the car. When my line is pulled,

I reel in hard. I want to show this fish the bright side
of the earth: a green-and-yellow dotted fish in my hand.

His mouth opens, closes, opens, closes, drops
blood on the snow. I watch his black eyes turning pink

slowly out here on the bright side of earth.

Lea Assenmacher

Remains

Shovels rise in darkness.
The grave on the riverbank under the weeping willows
was shallow, four feet deep, the bodies
brought in by cart and dumped.
Their shawls their shrouds.
At nightfall the doctors gathered,
drew lots, retrieved their prize.

One Who Stands On A Cloud, Dakotah warrior
        this fiend with human shape
lies upon the laboratory table.
With surgical precision Dr. Mayo
cuts open the abdomen, coldly
examines heart, belly, brain

in the name of science
        the mean cranial capacity of the skulls of Whites was 87 cubic inches
        based on the measurement of 144 skulls of Native Americans, he
        reported a figure of 82 in³

in the name of knowledge
> *in their mental character the Americans are averse to cultivation,*
> *and slow in acquiring knowledge; restless, revengeful, and fond of*
> *war, crafty, sensual, ungrateful, obstinate and unfeeling,*
> *and much of their affection for their children may be traced to*
> *purely selfish motives*

in the name of revenge
> *the Indian brain is so deficient that the race would be impossible*
> *to civilize*

and when he is done with the meat

he scrapes clean the bones
polishes them to gleaming whiteness
wires them together and hangs them
to teach his sons.

The skull of One Who Stands On A Cloud
sits on the doctor's desk
forty years.

— Otter Tail —

Candace Simar

Drought

We talked about the weather, the crops, and the cost of gasoline.
Complained about taxes, the price of wheat. Every conversation
a variation of the same. The women stitched feed sack dresses or
embroidered dishtowels and worried about the corn. The men cast
anxious glances towards the skies while monkeying with worn down
tractors or patching wagons with baling wire. We never talked about
feelings, never acknowledged emotions. We commented on "how
someone was taking" a death in the family, bragged about someone
who just kept working, the one who refused to let a little thing like
death or sickness get him down or set him back. We glossed over the

big things and dwelt in smaller places, closer in size to the acreage
of our farms. Maybe town people talked about deeper issues. We
didn't. When a neighbor shot himself, Auntie Ragna complained
at the funeral about the lack of butter on the egg salad sandwiches.
Old lady Norstrom trying to save a penny, she said, always trying
to squeeze another nickel out of every dime. No one mentioned the
suicide. No one talked to his boys, red and sodden in their Sunday
suits, other than a crisp nod and quick handshake. They held up
real well, Auntie would say later. Never shed a tear.

Scott King

The First Farms

Fallen barns, houses, sheds—
moss-heavy rafters, post and beam
broken, sinking into soil
like old shipwrecks.
                    Field stone,
a scattering of store-bought bottles,
hammer-and-anvil nails, rust—
the little that's left
lost among the roots
of returning ash, sugar
maple, oak, and elm.

Angela Foster

Where I'm From

I'm from butchering hens in the forenoon and eating fried chicken
for supper. Once a week baths and the old upright piano with the
middle C that clanged an empty thump. From forenoon coffee and
afternoon chores. Dinner at noon and supper after milking. Meat
and potatoes at every meal. Whole milk fresh from the bulk tank,

the cream rising to the top. From fried bacon, fried ham, fried steak, fried eggs, fried potatoes and Mom's homemade doughnuts. Beet pickles, head cheese, pickled pigs feet, dumpling soup, and cream and bread with a little sugar sprinkled on top. From cooking for the threshers and cooking for the silo fillers. *Crik*, not creek. *Swatter*, not swather. *Warsh*, not wash. *Not'n*, not nothing. From Norwegian swear words and a grandpa who drank, covering the smell with Sen-Sen candies. From Auntie Ruby with her tightly curled hair and house dresses, who pinched my cheeks with hands so chapped it hurt. From Great-Uncle Louie who chewed snus and always stuck out his finger for me to pull. And from fat Grandma Inga who warned me not to. I'm from lefse, krumkake and rhubarb gritty with soil, sour in my mouth. Ripe wheat chewed into gum. Apple pies, mud pies, and cow pies. The smell of manure and the suck of a baby calf's mouth. From hay bales that made you sneeze and straw of pure gold. From "Come Boss!" to the cows and "Sic 'em" to the dog. A two-holer outhouse and a one-room school house. Pump-Pump-Pullaway, Red-Rover, Red-Rover, and Anti-I-Over. Climbing trees, skipping stones, and hopscotch. From green hills and pastures dotted with hardwoods and rocks the size of melons heaved up in the soil. From dirt, dark as blackstrap molasses and crops sprouting like new hair in the spring fields. From coffee in a jar carried barefoot through the fields to my father's waiting hands. From salt and sweat and dirt-creased skin. From all of this. From home.

— Pennington County —

Charmaine Pappas Donovan

An Education in Thief River Falls

Newly married and introduced
to that ironed-on world, a river town
of my husband's boyhood high jinks,
I entered, at mid-year, radio broadcasting school

as a non-traditional student,
older than most members of the class.
I had the Class C License others desired;
classmates grinned as I misread gauges,
fumbled with dials, mispronounced *Quonset*.
They howled while watching me tangle
in the ropes of learning the hard way,
a tough obstacle course taught by Mr. Rokke.
While assigned evening "on air" time
only a certain long song by Gordon Lightfoot
or Led Zeppelin's *Stairway to Heaven*
made it possible to leave the microphone
and hightail it to a bathroom stall
at the end of the hall, those minutes
a safety net against the dread of dead air.
Listeners never knew why
instrumentals segued into news.
It was a gimmick we often used
rather than gauge the length of a song
or make it correspond precisely
to the fateful second-hand
sweeping twelve at the top of each hour.

I never looked back to the apartment
where we pounded hallway walls
to silence loud music after ten o'clock,
or how the stolen check from our mailbox
only proved the name of the town.
I forgot about black ice roads more slippery
than the slope of most marriages.
Here, I heard the beginning sputter of an engine,
glimpsed from the corner of my eye—
the silver shudder of a single-engine plane
stalled and headed for a flat open field,
my life spinning the hard way.

—Pine County —

Angela Foster

Farmer

The dirt—harsh, black and
peppered with rocks—
stuck to his work boots
like spring gumbo.

The green shoots
kept my father's
stubborn hope alive,
a fire licking twigs.

He said it a hundred times:
  after the rocks are picked
  after planting
  after harvest
next year.

Dirt kept him going long
after his body needed rest,
working the fields all night
on a rusty John Deere tractor,
soil embedded into
the wrinkles of his skin.

Dirt eroded his health like
a south wind through a dry field.

In the end, it was
the dirt that toppled him.
In his passing, the dirt
welcomed him home.

Nancy Paddock

Hell's Gate

All the little rain
falling here
in roaring shreds
through a narrow gap in rocks.

The Kettle River
is only water,
finding the lowest path
to the sea.

That one hollow between waves
where I cannot lay my body
without dying,

only eyes can touch.

I want this storm
flooding my veins,
washing my nerves.

I want to let go
and be pulled
by the Earth's weight down.

But my blood
is the only thunder in my ears,

a dry beating
at Hell's Gate.

Chris York

Pine City Blue

The crusted snow and deep winter twilight
is a blue, toward indigo, of heavy burdens.

Blue that descends like fog. Street lamps
flicker. Neon strains to glow.

A wilted blue smelling of Laundromats, haunting
alleyways like exhaust—hovering, casually toxic.

A blue of lethargic drives down lonely roads,
and wild-eyed shadows in the northern pines.

John Minczeski

Thaw

It is mire and muck down to the frost line,
all melt through the flooded fields;
an intermittent sky, encroaching woods
as I drive; every dip in the road's another culvert
through which the spring thaw shoots mud and sky
just this side of ice
swollen out of the muscles of snow
as the run-off grinds through sandstone,
more diamond than water.

At Pine City the river deserves its name
Snake, except it roars instead of rattles
as it twists and rolls like fire
drawing a million sirens towards its smoke
and calls a two-year old who waits
until his mother's back is turned.
Three weeks later the river's tame again.
The parents stand outside their cabin

saying to the reporters *he's gone back,*
he's just gone back. The newsmen
pause, the camera augers in.

The men in hip boots have given up dragging
and gone to hand-tied flies. How deaf I am, driving past
that moment the river wailed,
stampede bulging in the middle, tearing out
trees and banks, gnawing itself and craving
anything this once besides itself,
anybody's child.

— Pipestone County —

Michael Lange

I Remember

my first charge account well:
Ruby's popcorn stand
and the tough cash
flow of the paper route.
I leaned on her counter
ledge and rolled my bicycle tires
back and forth and smiled in at her
wide, red-cheeked smile
and hemmed and hawed and
finally just out asked.
I remember the first firm "yes"
and how she printed my name
and—10 cents—in her rainbow tablet.
Ruby made the best
popcorn I have ever eaten—
hot coconut oil popcorn
popped in a warm penny candy

closet on main street. Her trust
in my stomach was quick and sure.

When I heard that her heart
had put her in the hospital
and she could have no visitors
I rode over to her darkened house
and prayed under the moon and the
cottonwood chorus and windy clouds.

The last time I saw Ruby
she was in her garden
still with her apron on
carefully picking marigolds.
She declined my final payment
saying she wanted something
to remember me by and hoped
I would not go hungry
or ever get in over my head.

Lorraine Powell Erickson

Night in a Country Town Hospital

Through hushed halls, the telephone rings.
The nurse's voice betrays the calmness of her words.
"Come-at-once. It-could-be-serious."
Then from a different room, a newborn's first cry.
Another nurse's voice, "You have a son!"
While in between, the light and heavy footsteps fall.

Thus life begins, while death prowls in the hall
And in the dark, we sleep on, and we sleep on.

Leo Dangel

Stone Visions

Along Highway 23,
south of Jasper, Minnesota,
the stones in the fields
look like old women
on their hands and knees.
I'm pleased to discover
this feminine hold
on a rugged landscape.
The heads of prairie grasses
are brushing the flanks
of ancient grandmothers.
But I remember
driving this way long ago
with my uncle, a farmer.
On seeing the stony acres,
he, too, had a comment,
"I'd hate like hell
to start picking rock
in those fields."

— Polk County —

Charmaine Pappas Donovan

Snapshot of an October Afternoon

Plumes of trees
feather a humped horizon.
From the road
gray remnants of house

sag full of ghosts
and other spineless things.
Boarded windows
turn curious eyes inward:
their lids closed
against outside storms.

A fiery heat of woods
looms ready to lick
the abandoned dwelling
into a funeral pyre.
Yet feeble yellow grassland
on the verge of winter somnolence
holds a home
in its soft palm,
pillow for an old dreamer
knee deep in sleep.

— **Pope County** —

Bill Holm

A Circle of Pitchforks

*(A poem about the farmers' protest against a proposed
powerline through Pope County, Minnesota)*

I

They used to call it a sheriff's sale.
Had one over by Scandia in the middle of the Thirties.
My dad told me how
the sheriff would ride out to the farm
to auction off the farmer's goods for the bank.
Neighbors came with pitchforks

to gather in the yard:
"What am I bid for this cow?"
Three cents. Four cents. No more bids.
If a stranger came in and bid a nickel,
a circle of pitchforks gathered around him,
and the bidding stopped.
Even in the gray light of memory
the windmill goes around uneasily,
the farmer's overalls
blow into the fork tines,
the striped overalls look like convict suits.
A smell of cowshit and wet hay seeps into everything.
The stranger wears tweed clothes
and a watch chain.
The sheriff's voice weakens
as he moves from hayrack to hayrack
holding up tools,
describing cattle and pigs
one at a time.
The space between those fork tines
is the air we all breathe.

II

"Resist much, obey little."
Walt Whitman told us.
To bring the light!
That's the thing!
Somewhere in North Dakota
lignite gouged out of the prairies
is transformed into light.
But you are not in darkness, brothers,
for day to surprise you like a thief.
We are all sons of the light,
sons of the day;
we are not of the night,
or of darkness.
Let us not sleep, as others do
but keep awake and be sober.
Those who sleep,
sleep at night,

and those who get drunk,
are drunk at night.

III

There is so much light in Minnesota:
the white faces brought here from Arctic Europe,
the lines of white birch in the white snow,
white ice like a skin over the water,
even the pale sun seen through snow fog.
White churches, white steeples, white gravestones.

Come into an old café
in Ghent, or Fertile, or Holloway.
The air is steamy with cigarette smoke and frozen breath,
collars up under a sea of hats pulled down.
You can hardly see the mouths moving under them.
The talk is low, not much laughing.
Eat some hot dish, some Jello,
and have a little coffee and pie.
Those are the men wrecking the ship of state—
the carriers of darkness.
Up in the cities
the freeway lights burn all night.

IV

My grandfather came out of Iceland
where he took orders from the Danes and starved.
After he died, I found his homestead paper
signed by Teddy Roosevelt,
the red wax still clear and bright.
In the corner, a little drawing of a rising sun
and a farmer plowing his way toward it.
A quarter section, free and clear.
On his farm he found arrowheads
every time he turned the soil.
Free and clear. Out of Iceland.
In the thirties, the farm was eaten by a bank,
thrown back up when Olson
disobeyed the law that let them gorge.
In high school they teach

that Hubert Humphrey was a liberal
and Floyd Olson is a highway.

V

Out on the powerline barricades,
the old farmers are afraid their cows'
teats will dry up after giving strange milk,
and their corn will hum in the granary all night.

They have no science, no words, no law,
no eminent domain
over this prairie full of arrowheads and flowers,
only they know it,
and the state does not.

We homestead in our bodies too,
a few years, and then go back
in a circle
faster than the speed of light.

Anna Marie Larson

Dishes

Today at the cabin in my thirtieth year I'm washing dishes at the end
of winter and ice on the lake is nearly melted and the shore of it is
breaking on the rocks just like tinkling crystal, chimes echoing up
and down and piled in great white mounds as benign as soap suds.

The ice is speaking. Inside the glass I could want nothing more than
a night of dishes, the world's dishes in their hot bath eclipsing all
thoughts for the sake of this task. I'll let the tap run till it steams
before filling the old porcelain sink. Hot enough water cleans
without soap, but I want suds mounting into clouds, water hot
enough to hurt, to send shooting pains of love up my arms to startle
and station me there with my belly pressed against the edge of the
sink, elbows out, neck bowed like a defeated angel. I can't bear to

be so weak and here at the sink I can't bear not to be. My knees almost knock the cupboard.

Dirty dishes are every bit as dirty as I am with residues of days gone by without washing a dish. Some I've set to soak and that is good to prepare them a little. The casserole dish and the gravy boat, the pie pan, squash and bread loaf pans will be last to dirty the water. These are the best meals to clean up after since I want to be here for eternity—hours with nothing but going to bed left for the day. It could be my last! Nothing but scrubbing, sliding, washing and rinsing and setting dishes out to drip dry the whole length of the counter on clean white dish towels.

Sometimes there simply aren't enough dishes. Good china is fine. I'll be careful not to leave a trace of food or grease. I'll take care to rinse them front and back, appreciate the green Depression ware and the Japanese black clay pitcher and wide coffee cups. I'll get every trace of wine pressing fingers deep to the bottom of flutes and goblets. Let me wash the flower vases and the pottery on the shelves; they've only been dusted all these years and would love to be bathed in hot clean water. None of that quick washing to keep up everyday, swift washing on the way from one errand to another, hating every dish that passes through my hands.

Let a man love me washing dishes. He'll take me by surprise with a kiss on the neck and a hand sliding around my waist. He can put on some old blues or jazz and return to me, but he'll have to wait until I finish washing the dishes, because it's a little of my precious time to pick one thing up and set one thing down new and shining, to think of the day and lay it to bed.

— Ramsey County —

Diego Vázquez, Jr.

Airline Announcement

for tria

As a civilian not only did she stand down the general
she asked, over the announcement circuit,
loud, gentle as is her manner, yet with discipline and authority,
with inspiration that made you want to respond to her at once,
my sister said, standing in the sky on her airline, new as she was
   to the wings,
not understanding anything about the war in Asia, the one
already counting thousands of our teens and women and men,
to all the passengers:
Please write your congressmen to stop the war!

The report of this action almost cost her the job,
but the chains above, demanding and correcting
got her to insist that she was mistaken to have spoken
free speech on company time, so she flew on and flew
for thousands of thousands miles in the sky, already a
veteran of the war.

Diego Vázquez, Jr.

Borders

In Roseau
the Canadian
border
ten miles north
is becoming

almost
unbearable
for the MN residents
of Euro surplus
extraction
because
the aftermath
of the world trade
center collapse
has created
stoppages
when they must wait
almost five minutes
to cross on the return
to America.

I being Americano
of Chicano
extraction
offer no
sympathy
and without having to
say a word
the residents
understand my
lack of sensitivity
to their plight.

Lloyd Young

Mixed Voices

At the open door
of a store-front mission,
Ernest Bearheart blinks and stares
in the garish glare of neon
and summons strength
from the pit of hunger

in the pits of his despair.
A Salvation Army tambourine
recalls another drum—
drum and rattle, chanting,
dancing—so long ago
in a distant land
that he has since strayed from.
"Just a closer walk with thee …"
as Ernest enters in,
his inner spirit singing;
another meal, a place to sleep,
tomorrow a new beginning
and a promise hard to keep.
"Let it be, Dear Lord, let it be!"

Evelyn Klein

Scent of Leaves

seagulls
stroke
over battle creek pond
as if it were the ocean
playfully loop the sky
crisscross

in annual
autumn maneuver
geese
gather
on the feather-littered meadow
each side of the path
walk in rows
like children on a rope

breath
of a new season

ducks
spread out
leisurely
on the pond
like the people hiking
in pairs or alone
or fishing

Mike Hazard

Snow Job

Shoveling black Tiger Jack's white snow
in the midst of the first blizzard of the season,
I thought about how he prefers to call himself a Negro.
I scraped and skimmed the concrete thought, row on row.
When I was almost through, it was time to start again.
Black and white, like a wise crow in the snow.
Black and white, history deeper than deepening snow.
Black and white, the photos tell us old stories
of civil rights and uncivil wrongs, of heroines and heroes.
Shoveling black Tiger Jack's white snow
in the midst of the first blizzard of the season,
I thought about how he prefers to call himself a Negro.

Mrs. H.E.B. M'Conkey

The Temperance Watchman

God speed your heaven-born efforts, ye high-souled noble band;
And crown with signal victory, the labors of your hand,
You're marshaled for the contest in glorious array,
And onward speed the conquest, till victors of the day.

The little germ entrusted unto the fruitful earth,
Has taken deep root downward, and rose in beauteous birth;
The fragile acorn first appears, and then abroad expands,
And soon the stately oak doth wave, the glory of the lands.

This tiny fragrant rose-bud first smiles upon its stem
Then bursts into gloomy petals, to gladden hearts of men:
It yields a sacred influence to all within its sphere—
Exhales a grateful perfume through all the tainted air.

God help the noble watchman to fight king Alcohol,
Until they close each "rum shop," and each "saloon" and "hall,"—
To send abroad their influence throughout this fair domain,
Until from our escutcheon is wiped its darkest stain.

— Red Lake County —

Doris Lueth Stengel

Small Town Lines

Embroidered dishtowels circumscribed
women's lives: Monday, Wash Clothes;
Tuesday, Iron. In the early 1960's
young housewives felt judged
by how early and how spotless
their laundry appeared on backyard lines,
especially in towns like Plummer.

Tea towels commanded: on Sunday
We Go To Church and most citizens did.
Shoulder to shoulder on one block,
four variegated churches in town
faced south (pioneers remembering
to face doors away from icy Alberta
Clippers roaring in from the northwest).

In a budget of large families' chores,
football and basketball practice
took second place to cow milking.
Girls tended large gardens
(come August cellar shelves bulged
with womanly jars of beans and peas).
Fathers usually said what came next.

The east-west gravel Main Street
was marked on the east by the elevator,
on the west by the Creamery along banks
of the Red Lake River. Wedged between,
a locker plant, bowling alley,
Mott's Hardware and DuChamps Grocery.
Orderly life was aligned by the dictums

of muslin towels that wore out too soon
from daily use, surviving as dust cloths
and scrub rags in a practical after-life.
Sunday held simple pleasures: picnics
and town baseball, evenings with the Cartwrights—
all eyes strained to watch Hoss and Little Joe lope
across multi-gray ranges of 12-inch TVs.

Sharon Chmielarz

Birch Trees

The birch stand in uneven rows of black and white,
their translation of soft rain falling.

Their vertical script, older than the fifth century,
younger than the birth of the Mississippi,

precursor to haiku and tanka, their shadows stressed
by the brush of a crow's wing. They've mastered

image and impression. Their genius is to capture
silence and space, from left or right, up or down.

What seems backwards among them moves forward.
No language is sure how or why this moves.

—Redwood County —

Joe Paddock

Frogs

At that time there was still a pothole
over every hill and the frogs in the fall
swarmed like maggots in the carcass of a dead horse.
Sometimes, after the coming of the cars,
they had to get out the blade to scrape the slick
of crushed frogs off that road that circles Stork Lake.

One sunny Saturday afternoon in late September,
more than forty years back now,
down around the bay,
about fifteen town kids began to herd frogs
up from the water's edge where they lay
dozing in the sun by the thousands,
big heavy leopard frogs that would stretch
nine, ten inches from nose to toe claw.

They herded them slowly
up over Anderson's pasture hill.
You would've thought it was wind through grass
sweeping ahead of them.
Herded them up onto the road into town,
herded them with real care, losing a few here and there,

but maintaining the mass
(some guessed five thousand, some ten),
and at the corner of Sixth,
they turned them, losing maybe forty dozen
which bounced on over Hershey's lawn,
confusing the bejesus out of their old Basset hound, Monty,
who, after sniffing and poking with his paw,
sat down and howled at a thin silver sliver
of day moon in the sky.

Old Mrs. Angier said she first heard a sound
like five thousand hands patting meat,
and when she looked up the street, she saw
these kids, serious and quiet, with a grey-brown wave,
like swamp water to their knees,
rolling along in front of them.

Mrs. Angier said, "Now, you never heard a word
from a single one of those kids.
They were silent and strange with that haze of a wave
rolling along in front of them.
Just that patting sound
times five thousand.
I tell you, it made goose flesh roll
up my back and arms!"

The boys claimed later that they had no plan,
but, when they came alongside "Horse" Nelson's
Fixit Quick Garage—which contained
maybe a half dozen broken-down cars
and "Horse" and Allen, his son, and "Windy" Jeffers—
one kid barked: "Bring 'em on in!"
and they turned that herd of frogs on a dime
(they were herding easy by that time),
and ran them through the entranceway.
Young Jim Hedeen grabbed the handle
of the sliding door and rolled her shut,
and those kids vanished like fifteen rabbits
into whatever weed patch they could find.

Well, hell, you can imagine.
"Windy" was on his back working upward on a spring

when those slimy devils started sliding all over him.
They say he most-near tipped that Model A on its side
getting out of there. And "Horse,"
who was no doubt nearly through his daily pint
of peach brandy, dropped a cam shaft
on Allen's toe and ran and hid in the can,
and Allen, who'd been mean and noisy
from his first squawk on, began hopping one-footed
amidst that froth of frogs. (And you *know*
how they have a way of climbing
up the inside of your pants, all wet
and with those scratchy little claws!)
Allen, slam-banging whatever came to hand,
tipped a couple cars from jacks, and screamed:

"I'M GONNA GET KEVIN KLIMSTRA FOR THIS!"

Forty-three years have passed,
but those frogs have never quit rolling
from the tongues of people around town.
It's one of those stories you learn early
and carry with you, and measure
the taste of life by
till the day you die.

Nancy Paddock

The Machine That Changed Winter

Within their fortresses of noise
snarling snowmobiles
snake among trees,
leaving a wake of tank tracks,
overrunning birdsong
and the trickling sounds of thaw,
grinding over the last defense
of bushes,
claiming the park for technology.

and sparrow wings lightly
brush snow shadows
from a black branch

They swarm,
black and yellow Scorpions from Mars,
Panthers, Arctic Cats in a continual leap
for the throat,
a hunger
that never connects
drawn out into winters
of discontented growling.

    and the white stag playfully
    rubs his antlers
    on the buffalo's shaggy head
    fenced-in
    because they are wild

When they stop,
they leave their machines
running
and stand faceless
in black vinyl,
yelling at each other
in the roar,

sounds
enough like machine gunfire
to set their minds at peace.

Loraine Schwanke Mueller

Portrait of Pioneers

They came in covered wagons from the east
and found the land of Minnesota good;
both Scandinavians and Germans pieced
their quilts from scraps in every neighborhood.
The sod-huts dotted prairies, sometimes wore

a daisy-crown from seeds imbedded there.
Though primitive, their lives were not a bore;
young children must be taught to read and share.
From Arrowhead and trading posts far north
to central plains and farmlands south and west,
they built log cabins and somehow brought forth
abundant water, meat and fish. They blessed
the One who brought them through great trials here,
and we, in turn, bless every Pioneer.

— Renville County —

Phebe Hanson

Cinderella

After your mother turns to stone,
you sit beside your father
in the high Model A,
driving to church in the country.
You sit in the front row,
singing hymns in Norwegian
to please him.

At home in the kitchen
you make Eggs Goldenrod
for him and your other children,
laughing as you blow crumbled yolks
at each other.

You are as good and as beautiful
as your mother.
Secretly you smile to yourself:
he needs no other wife.

When summer comes, you lie
aching and peeling with Scarlet Fever.

A hired woman brings you meals in bed.
You can go nowhere with him for weeks.

He heads his car away
from your quarantined house,
finds another to replace you.
Later, the new mother smiles
down at you from the high front seat,
while you climb into the back
with the other children.

Phebe Hanson

Sacred Heart

In Sacred Heart, Minnesota,
we Lutherans
barely knew the Catholic kids.
Their mothers smoked Camels,
played bridge in the afternoons
instead of Ladies' Aid.
Their fathers, lying under their Chevvies,
said, *goddamn*, cursing the motors to life.

But we build bird baths of cement,
pressed splinters of broken bottles
into their wet breasts.
Hosiery salesmen driving through
to the Cities marveled.
We gave hoboes
who asked at our backdoors for food
glasses of buttermilk
because it was good for them.

When I was eight, a big Catholic kid asked me
up to his garage loft to see his crucifix.
Even then I knew that Lutherans are justified
by faith alone,
and kept my legs crossed.

Larry Gavin

After Reading Tu Fu I Go Off to Catch Rough Fish In the Cannon River

"The river carries off the moon
To set beyond the border." Tu Fu

Together, carp gather like shadows in the slack
current—moving like dark thoughts through
the moon's shadow. We are joined by a line
the exact thickness of desire: a line that stretches
into current moving below the surface in ways
only the moon understands; pulled by its fullness
to extremes that become more than only the Cannon
River. That become all rivers stretching the borders
of what I know for a fact to be true. In the settling
darkness—me, the moon, this carp all balance on
the sudden edge of daylight and dark. All the while
doing my best to stay connected.
                                                    When the fish
comes to hand in the shallows, offering itself
like the answer to some question that I don't
recall asking, I handle it gently. Then let it go.

Larry Gavin

Conversation with a Girl Sculpting a Fist: Faribault Area Learning Center

With the nightly news as a background
and as if I am not there, you say when you
were growing up there was never money
for food. You were thirteen before you
tasted butter.

                Your fingers are creating
fingers, creating veins on a wrist and then
knuckles: like saying to your mother
"I'll be right there." But instead
you say, "This war. There is a darkness
that will last my whole life. Killing
is killing it doesn't matter who is doing
it or why."
                The evening news shows a boy
not much older than you coming home
from war, and in the shadow behind him
there is the darkness he brings home
with him, and that you must live with.
                            And your sister
had to move to Arizona and you
miss her, you say, so much, because for years
it was just the two of you. And in summers
when the power died in the dark heart
of a thunderstorm, you sisters hugged
each other on the living room floor.
The name, you said, gave you hope.
Surrounded in the darkness by a circle
of flashlights gathered all day against
the news of bad weather.
                        The fist is a fist now.
Tomorrow, you say, when it is fired,
you hope it won't explode.

Scott King

Peace Agreement

It's morning, the light still messy. Birdsong like tattered curtains
     on the day's window.
He takes the old card-table (the one with the cigarette burns) into
     the backyard.
Shadows fall across it like streaked linen. Folding chairs and place
     settings are laid for each leader, each warring faction.

It's quiet and the wind in the trees like a whisper passing through an
audience.
No one comes. He pours a glass of lemonade.
Moisture condenses and drips down the side of his glass.
The shadows retreat, go somewhere. He waits.
A butterfly passes by. And then a bee.

Scott King

Restoring the Prairie

Wanting to recreate the Great Plains, he clears one corner of his
backyard.
Ornamental shrubs are cut down. Lilies dug up.
He listens to the sound the shovel makes. And each time he presses
it into the earth he hears a burning match quenched in water.
Out of his pocket he takes great handfuls of seed and fluff gathered
on long walks into the country and the past.
He sows thistle, goldenrod, prairie grasses big and small, asters and
smoke.
Where long ago a fenceline stood, he plants chokecherries, wild
plum, hazelnuts. Later,
from his porch, he watches and waits and imagines—quite confident
blue sky, prairie hawk, buffalo will all return.

Marie Vogl Gery

Without a Full Moon
July 5, 2007

Last Saturday under the full moon
two baby robins overflowed their nest outside the window
wild daylilies splashed orange at the edge of the woods

In the grocery store a young mother

held her baby, hair thick and black as raven feathers
Tu bebe es mas bonita—Gracias
¿Como se nombre?—Es un niño
¿ Como se llama?—Es Oscar
Ah, no es bonita. Es muy guapo.—Si, si

Each night people cross the Sonoran desert
Tied together by fear and a rope
they walk North for a better life
knowing, not knowing, hoping

Each week death counts rise
Lucresia identified only by silver rings on her fingers
Under the mesquite a dead mother holds her son
Alone Alfonso lies on a small hill
Women, men, children dehydrated
defeated by heat and distance

Far from where I have been for months I walk and walk
call down the powerful voice of the bullfrog in the pond
ask the gods for the cardinal's whistle, the robin's tenacity pulling worms
plead for the strength of the wind, the coolness of rain
the light of the sun, the wisdom behind the stars
the courage to declare as a mother
we belong, all of us, to the one family of earth

— Rock County —

Freya Manfred

Blue Mound, Luverne, Minnesota

> *They say all is one instantaneously at any given moment:*
> *past, present, and future—so, if true, where is time …?*
> *—Frederick Manfred, Sr.*

> *You were not a house, not a home; but a sanctum,*
> *my refuge, an island of innocence.*
> *—Frederick Manfred, Jr.*

Purple buffalo berries and yellow mullein bloom amid flowing grasses
and flesh-colored boulders tall as church steeples.
I was married here by Eagle Rock.
Before that I ran away to write poems.
Before that I dreamed of finding my future somewhere else
while a ring of black and white cows gathered to watch me sleep.
Before that settlers built sod huts and plowed fields of corn.
Before that Lakota braves ran buffalo off the quartzite cliffs for food.
Before that flower and grass seeds sprouted in the prairie winds.
I want to die looking out over these farms and fields,
by the old rocks and under the new sky.

Freya Manfred

Green Pear Tree in September

On a hill overlooking the Rock River
my father's pear tree shimmers,
in perfect peace,
covered with hundreds of ripe pears
with pert tops, plump bottoms,

and long curved leaves.
Until the green-haloed tree
rose up and sang hello,
I had forgotten …
He planted it twelve years ago,
when he was seventy-three,
so that in September
he could stroll down
with the sound of the crickets
rising and falling around him,
and stand, naked to the waist,
slightly bent, sucking juice
from a ripe pear.

Mike Hazard

Rare Birds

As soon as Frederick Feikema Manfred flew off
to address a waitress he believes has the best lips
in the county and who was probably avoiding him,
the man in the next booth turned to our table
and said with pride he's read the author's every book.
Mr. Manfred paused to talk to him on the rebound,
and confided to us he always takes the time to talk
with the man because readers are such rare birds.
Then old Fred sniffed like he'd never sniffed before,
and his arm, like the wing of a great eagle, feathered
the entire chicken, rib and steak-chewing restaurant
as he stated, "Not many of these people read."

146

— Roseau County —

Karsten Piper

Down Highway 11

My daughters sleep. Their breathing sings,
the engine hums. The pavement tickers under,
the centerline strings past below my arm,
stretches, and disappears ahead.
Our dash lights glow, our radio is silent.
The world lies dark, continuous and flat
     until the skyline leaps a thousand
fathoms over Warroad, horizon
reels out into shore, every cloud
is suddenly reflection skimming on
unmeasured blue-black water.
Eleven plunges to the coast, the future
comes, no vanishing point stays put
for long. I drive us down, the girls asleep,
their open mouths breathe in the sea.

Annette Hermansen

Three Haiku:

Determination

Neon green tree frog
   clings to broken branch—
      fearful, but stubborn

Jane's Generosity

Plump blackberries plucked
one by one from forest's edge,
just enough to share.

On Guard

A large, handsome gull
claims for himself the whole lake—
well-fed, but alone.

—St. Louis County —

Connie Wanek

April

When the snow bank dissolved
I found a comb and a muddy quarter.
I found the corpse of that missing mitten
still clutching some snow.

Then came snow with lightning,
beauty with a temper.
And sleet, the compromise that pleases no one;
precipitation by committee.

Out on Lake Superior the worried ice
paces up and down the shoreline
wearing itself out.

Chimneys have given up smoking.
In the balcony of the wood,
a soprano with feathers.

And upon the creek
the wicked spell is broken.
You are free to be water now.
You are free to go.

Connie Wanek

Duluth, Minnesota

A moose has lost his way
amidst the human element downtown,
the old timers waiting out January
at the bar, the realtors and bureaucrats
with their identical plumage
(so that you must consult your Roger Tory Peterson)
hopping up the steps of City Hall
eating Hansel's bread crumbs—
poor moose, a big male who left
his antlers somewhere in the woods.
He keeps checking his empty holster…

People suffer the winters
for this kind of comedy.
Spectators climb the snow banks,
dogs bark, the moose lowers
his shaggy head, his grave eyes
reminiscent somehow of Abe Lincoln.
Firemen, police, reporters, DNR,
two cents worth from every quarter,
till the moose lopes down Fourth Street
toward St. Mary's Hospital Emergency Entrance
and slips into an alley.

Later, the same moose—it must be—
is spotted farther up the hillside.
It's a mixed neighborhood; a moose
isn't terribly out of place.
And when he walks calmly up behind
an old man shoveling his driveway,
the Duluthian turns without surprise:
Two blocks east, he says,
Then you'll hit a small creek that will take you
to Chester Park, and right into the woods.
He adds, *Good luck, now.*

Gary Boelhower

Hawks Ridge

On Hawks Ridge I watch the ancient
pilgrimage. They follow the high
road of water shimmer and wind race,
each feather gorged with air
and their wings cupping the blue
silence like sleek swimmers.
Some come gliding in, banking
on currents, hanging on thermals,
knowing the sweet surrender
of the whole body given and taken.
Others fall like hungry stones
out of the sky, eyes trained, cruel
talons ready to caress the warm
pulsing body of survival.

I come here to dream of air
and the long canyons of luminescence,
to unshackle my body from the earth,
hacksaw the chains with long
cuts of October wind and then glide
on a zephyr of lapidary light.

Unfetter me from the delusion
of destination, teach me to trust migration,
moon pull on the marrow in my bones.

Stephanie N. Johnson

Here and There

I seldom take the change.
But next time I will. Every penny or two
for little hands wanting a purse full of treasures.
Now that my daughter is growing lithe,

her voice stretches to meet the wind.
Beginning to speak is like this—
we're transferred through words to the lake.
Fur ball from the black cat heading
in that direction too. All the water flowing
from these hills into that basin. On to
the sea. From here, how many miles?
A thousand pitchforks triggered
in the mind. A million strands of hay
drying in the barn. Hair matted in the plastic brush.
Why bother pretending these things
are easily separated.

Loren Niemi

Hibbing

In the town where I was born the scarred
earth could always be seen, the bloody
slag piles, the boom and bust on the fortunes of steel
making mountains where molehills once stood.

My father's and a thousand other fathers'
childhoods carried away in ore cars
to feed American progress while
the mines devoured the ground where houses stood.

If I were there, I'd join the crawl
up First and down Howard
behind the wheel of a souped-up hot rod
capable of speed but rumbling in second gear.

Nowhere to go, nothing to do,
my cousins boil the night away with unnamed desire
to graduate and leave looking for anything
that is not this town, this work, this life, this fear.

If I were there, I might not be so lucky—
end up supporting a family for union wages

measuring time by the mine whistle
in a land dying but never quite dead.

Never quite rich, still restless and working
for retirement and the cabin on the lake or
a kid's college education like the one I'm getting
because my old man left that town long ago.

Connie Wanek

Ice Out

The south wind discovers a loose thread
and winter begins to unravel.
The first black and blue butterfly
materializes. The second.
They find each other.

The snow fort is in ruins.
Stacks of ammunition
have melted into the grass.
A float plane with stiff wings
banks over the pines, turning north;
an eagle, too, searches for open water.

Open water. A window to the bottom.
Sometimes the water is so clear
that it hardly exists
except as a change in viscosity.
The island has its moat again,
the moon its mirror.

— Scott County —

Ruth Brin

Boiling Springs

Water is essential to life everywhere, but nowhere more than in the desert. When Isaiah calls, "All who are thirsty, come and drink," he is speaking of faith in a metaphor of great meaning to a desert people. "Boiling Springs" is a real place in Minnesota.

The rain falls in summer on my green hill.
It trickles through layers of soil and sand
Through caverns and rocks below the land
To rivers unknown, in darkness and chill.

The waters above meet the waters below
Rushing unheard through the caverns of stone
Dropping and flowing in places unknown
Except for one pond, one spring that I know.

There at the foot of the quiet green hills
The waters boil up in the light of day
And run to the river a few miles away
To float the barges and power the mills.

I look at the pond which is never the same.
The waters were low some years, some high;
But my spring bubbled on, it never went dry,
The water was there whenever I came.

These waters will rise through soil and shale
Though the hills are brown and the grass dried hay.
Though the sun burn the earth day after day,
I believe: these waters will never fail.

Frances March Davy

Perversity

Why do I always wish
For other things—
For Indian Summer's smoky haze
In quiet Springs?

Why do I want the gentian's blue
Instead of hepatica's silvery hoods?
Why do I want the grebe's call?
Why do I long for Autumn woods?

Why do I always want some other thing?
In Spring the Fall,—in Fall the Spring.

— **Sherburne County** —

Claire van Breemen Downes

A Wish for My 120th Birthday

If still the eagles soar beyond the trees
that edge the water where the last ice cracks
and jostles as the river shrugs and frees
itself of winter; if the fragile wax
of bloodroot hides deep in spring's moist-moss wood,
and columbine comes venturing in June;
if doe and fawn may stand where once they stood
when we could watch, that evening all in tune;
if birches still may shimmer forth in green
and lilacs keep their old familiar scent—
if these remain, then I may sleep serene,
nor wake to wonder where our moment went.

Canary tokens, these, of life and breath—
their total is a greater sum than death.

If now your cities, hived and busy, gleam
clean-swept and sunlit, joyous and secure,
as alabaster as the patriot's dream,
as radiant, undimmed, as angel-pure—
where no child cries unhushed, unloved, unfed;
no women hide their bruises and are shamed;
where roses are as daily as the bread,
and laughter rises, and no one is blamed;
where parks are April-green and flower-bright,
where none will ever know the bitter rain
of fire bombs or missiles, or the sight
of wounded bodies or the sound of pain—
then I shall have no promises to keep
and, resting, I shall smile soft in my sleep.

Mary Willette Hughes

Late May

Morning has come beyond
the bedroom window
and High Bush cranberries lift
their flat-plate of buds:
round, clustered,
and randomly birthed
among thick serrated leaves.
See, already the circular
edge is laced
with white-blossoms.
We wait
for this season
of life to turn.
We wait
for a full-flowered feast
to be offered

tomorrow and tomorrow;
our eyes hunger
for rich, ripe berries
dangling in the sun
like rubies.

— Sibley County —

Gordon Anderson

Elegy for the Last Pioneer

the quarters in my hand rise
in the dim light of this bar
like autumn moons.

there are enough for groceries
enough for a few more beers
before I head home.

I am the last of this Catholic family.
forgotten by my brothers and sisters,
I live alone
with my mother.
my father's bones have flowered
in the earth.
the land he worked
turned to dust,
nests for the mudhens.

Mother, listen: my hands are barren.
I cannot fill my father's shoes.
I cannot make the wheat
gleam white in the morning air.

Chet Corey

Pursuit

Trains don't stop for Blakely.
Just three pulls on the horn
and the freight blows through—
seven cars and no caboose.
The scrape, like knife blade
on grindstone, of wheel on rail
and the only dog in town quiets.
The boarded-up saloon demands
your patronage as the river mine.

A caravan of bikers in leather
takes the bridge toward Green Isle.
The brown Minnesota is a glut
of gold elm leaf and sandbar—
blurred signatures of drought.
A rifle cracks two—four times
down river where deer forage.
Dry leaves gather into islands
in gravel beside the car.

You bring gifts in both hands—
yellow molars of corn and chaff
from beside the grain elevator
to sift through finger slits.
I pocket the kernels of corn
for blackbirds at my feeder,
and we drive toward Henderson
with the dream of café coffee.

— Stearns County —

Bill Meissner

After our 30th Birthdays, My Wife and I Walk to the Center of the Lake

This winter is always too long.

We brush away powdery snow: ice,
a foot thick but still clear.

We think we can see to the bottom
where minnows circle, fireflies in a jar,
where small pages of light are turning.

We love the simplicity of this ice;
if only we could always see this way—

we crouch down on hands and knees
like children peering at the world
through their first magnifying glass.

Joyce Sutphen

Bookmobile

I spend part of my childhood waiting
for the Stearns County Bookmobile.
When it comes to town, it makes a
U-turn in front of the grade school and
glides into its place under the elms.

It is a natural wonder of late
afternoon. I try to imagine Dante,
William Faulkner, and Emily Dickinson
traveling down a double lane highway
together, country-western on the radio.

158

Even when it arrives I have to wait.
The librarian is busy, getting out
the inky pad and the lined cards.
I pace back and forth in the line,
hungry for the fresh bread of the page,

because I need something that will tell me
what I am; I want to catch a book,
clear as a one-way ticket, to Paris,
to London, to anywhere.

Joyce Sutphen

Comforts of the Sun

To someone else these fields would be exotic:
the small rows of corn stretching straight
as lines of notebook paper, curving slightly over
the rise of a hill; the thick green

of the oatfields, which I could predict
would turn into the flat gold of summer straw;
the curled alfalfa, slung like a jacket
over the shoulder of horizon.

To someone else, the small groves of trees
along the barbed-wire fence would look like
shrines to a distant god, little remnants
of woodland standing against the tilling hand.

Someone else would need to be told
that my footprints, in a hundred different
sizes, are etched under layers of gray
silt at the center of the farmyard,

that bits of my father's skin are plowed
into every acre. They would have
to be told how I know each tree,
each rock too heavy to lift.

Joyce Sutphen

Homesteading

Long ago, I settled on this piece of mind,
clearing a spot for memory, making a
road so that the future could come and go,
building a house of possibility.

I came across the prairie with only
my wagonload of words, fragile stories
packed in sawdust. I had to learn how
to press a thought like seed into the ground;

I had to learn to speak with a hammer,
how to hit the nail straight on. When
I took up the reins behind the plow,
I felt the land, threading through me,
stitching me into place

Bill Meissner

Hometown Widow Whose Laundry Never Gets Clean

She's had enough of this town,
so she paints all the windows
of her house black.

She was tired of her neighbors' voices
scratching against the glass,
tongues filed hard
as the points of butcher knives.
Tired of always watching
for first snow, the way it smothers
her fingerprints on the begonias.

The quilted robe she wraps around herself is solitude.
This is the cloister no one can visit_
except the preacher on Sunday radio,

church music flying the hallway,
a canary with one wing.

She will go outside only to hang another load
of her dead husband's shirts on the line.
Through a fingernail crescent in the
kitchen window, she sees one hanger
blow off. The others on the line
bob nervously, black
wire frowns waiting
as the wind un-
hooks them
one by
one.

Edith Rylander

Minnesota, October Thirtieth

If I were a little lighter I could fly
The way brown oak leaves fly this scuttering day,
Over the stubble of corn and the cut hay,
And bone-bare trees against a cobalt sky.
The sun is glorious, but the wind is wry,
And summer's green is a long time blown away.
Grasshoppers buried in leaves hoard one more day
Their little sap before frost sucks them dry.
Wind scours me empty as the round calm eye
Of some old headbone, used and thrown away
In a field edge where stones have weathered gray.
If I were a little lighter I could fly.

— Steele County —

Jeanette Hinds

The Last Unlocking

Mother never threw a key away;
her top kitchen drawer jangled
      where they slid about.
Often she stood before a building in the sun
leafing through key after key after key.

To simplify life, I finally
ringed the tops with colored plastic:
green for shed housing the Snapper and Gilson,
red for granary holding Mission Oak chairs,
pink for garage and the Rambler
      that no longer ran,
purple for basement full of paint cans and jars
yellow for the back door to the house.

Every evening, moving building to building,
she double-checked each lock.

She could never have imagined the auction:
strangers loading her bed into a pickup, or
carrying off pictures, ladders, cream cans—
and as the sun began to set,
all doors standing open,
      empty
      like startled mouths.

Jeanette Hinds

Meditation on a Plow

Rotted hitching-tongue, rusted plowshares,
spokes and hubs of unturned wheels
weather under brittle weeds. Once
     the plow broke loam into furrows;
     turned earth ready for planting.

Soon each hill of corn stood separate
like green yarn tying a black quilt.
Stretching through four-cornered wind,
morning mist, July sun, each stalk
     tasseled by late summer,
     swelled with ears of corn.

In September, green silk dried to brown,
kernels dented, dry stalks rustled at touch.
Slow-driving a wagon through the rows,
we broke ears loose with pegs on our wrists,
stripped the husks, tossed the yellow corn
into the wagon—fitted with a "bang-board"
so we couldn't over-throw.

Now I too am a plow:
        turning soil upside-down,
        making earth ready for planting,
        earning the rust when my day comes
        to lie near a slatted corncrib
        where each year the yellow
        of another crop shows through.

— Stevens County —

Athena Kildegaard

Barns

stand at the edge of fallow fields,
beside tipped silos, soil rising against them,
sky pouring through collapsed eaves,
shingles strewn along field stone foundations,
chamfered braces hung with hornets' pipes.
How brazen they are, their splined floor boards
warped above splintered sleepers,
slash marks faded on oak-pegged beams,
manure in the byres leached and mealy.
They smell of solitude, of wood and iron
sawed by wind, of pigeons roosting on a lintel,
prickle bushes rooted in the stalls, of outside turned in.

Tom Hennen

Animal of the Earth

For the first time I understand
I'm an animal
Bones
Warm breath.
Moving shaggy arms
To encircle another.
Looked at
By beasts
That fly
Walk with four feet down
Crawl
On tiny scales that shine like flecks of spring.

I'm
The only animal
That wants to write a book
That moves so uncertainly through the cold
That spends so much time
Gazing at the sky
That listens for itself
Among the rustling sounds.

Tom Hennen

**Out of Work More Than a Year
Still No One Answers
My Letters of Application**

In late winter
Afternoon sunlight
Doesn't budge the snowbanks
That have fallen whole into the backyard.

A forecast for more cold.
On the edge of the roof
Icicles are in deep conversation.
I pretend I belong and start talking.

Vicki Graham

Winter's Edge

Prairie town: snow and thaw,
snow and thaw. Torn leaves
scratch iron earth, wrap
the trunks of elm and walnut and ash,
while March winds gnaw
dry grass, rip bark ragged as burlap.

The houses crouch, turn
blind eyes to the streets,
but the tips of the maples burn
red, the willows gold,
and along the river, winds rake
snow into patterns
complex as the curves
in Japanese sand gardens.
Outside town, the stiff grids
of roads and sidewalks falter.
Cattails rattle and shift by the lake.
Ice ribbons unwind along banks
picked clean by winter,
and the bronze stalks of milkweed,
bluestem, and porcupine grass
tangle and feather like frayed silk. Seeds
scattered in September heat wait
under filigreed snow that breaks
from white to rainbow
in late afternoon sun.
On the ridge, the windmill spins
wings sleek as a heron's
and the ethanol plant's smoke smudge thins
to silver threads dropped
over the town tucked against glacial till
where brittle lawns replace the prairie's gentian,
golden rod, aster, and meadow rue.

— Swift County —

Anne Marie Larson

Funeral Whites

The last one to the church—
Younger version of you, Grandmother—
Late like a bride kissing
Too long before the wedding, tasting her heaven
Bright on this Earth with us
Before anyone declared it proper,
As it was before anyone

Felt your radiance when the ethereal family rose
Over the chancel around your coffin and the heavy
Family in the front row felt something soaring,
Something pulling them open, out to the top
Of the chapel—Late because I needed new white
Undergarments for my white funeral dress.

Late because there was the detour through new fields.
At the turn into town maybe you told my hand to switch
The radio to a.m. You must have been there because two
Men announced your graduation, saying your full name.
Then you met me between the church and your house—
Late to your own funeral, your white coach passed me.

But there was one woman who never smiled.
You'd think she would have understood
The joy on my face. Her daughter had left her
Too soon, lost her Sarandon curls early
And her big eyes grew heavy and confused.
That mother wouldn't smile before the dead
And I couldn't keep from your radiance.

— Todd County —

Edith Rylander

Dream Warriors

Two country boys at work tearing a barn down,
Knocking down birds' nests, letting the sky in
Between old rafters. They have bared to the sun
Their teenaged muscles and pale northern skin,
And the chubby one that's going into the Army
Gets burned by noon. They work in a thundering bubble,
With portable screaming backbeat company,
A "You can't touch me" armor of rock and roll

That will blast them down back roads past thin farm acres
Gone back to popple. Past barns where turkeys stand
Wing to flightless wing in their dumb thousands,
Stuffing and staring till the packer's truck comes.
On a rusty oil tank next to the turkey barn, someone
Has spray-painted "Class of '88. Dream Warriors,"
But never said what sort of dream it is,
Nor what the weapons are, nor where the war.

The great world sings to boys. They hug their music
As if the enemy is that breathing stillness
Of roots expanding, and the wren's small tune
Melodiously defending the stick nest
Of gone and yet to come wren generations.
No jobs for young men here. They join the Army,
Or go gut turkeys in the packing house,
Taking their music, leaving the fields empty.

Ryan Kutter

How to Eat Raspberries

You'll come at the canes
with the idea of gorging yourself,
swallowing this rare vision of plenty.
A beginner's mistake, but go ahead.

Sit down in the thorn of them,
grasp all the clusters you can reach
before turning over the leaves.
Turning over the leaves is very clever.

Some berries aren't quite ripe,
but as close to it
as you are to understanding anything.
Eat them with the others.

When your belly roils with uncertainty
sit back. Lie down, even if spiders and slugs
are in the grass, lie down. Next time
bring a bucket. Bring them home.

I've eaten berries this way for years.

Edith Rylander

Maple-Tapping Song

After those years of drought
When we left the trees alone
We've decided to tap again.
Get out the spiles and buckets.
(There is no easy sweetness.)
Haul in plenty of dry wood,
Wash up the jugs and lids.

Days in the forties, nights
In the twenties, that's when the sap flows.
The bit grinds in through gray bark,
The sap goes "tunk!" in the pail.
Blue sky and chickadees singing,
Cold feet and geese going over,
And we make what prayer it is in us to make
In thanks for the blood of trees.

Wood smoke from dawn to past darkness,
Smells of sap and snow melting.
The eyes of the cat in sap-shack dark
Keeping warm by the crackle and glow.
Labor of glaciers and maples,
Golden-brown and thick when it's done.
Sweat a few weeks in sap time,

All the year round, eat the sun.

David Bengtson

The Masses

The 4'x8' sheet of plywood is supported by two stakes and planted next to a cornfield on the back road to Freeport so those approaching the intersection where the Rock Tavern is located can see the names of area Catholic churches and the times when masses are held. The white background and black lettering are fading. But what has stayed the same since the day the sign was painted is the name of the church at the bottom of the list—the seventh church—the one that might be missed by those in a hurry—the most controversial church of all—the one called Our Lady of the Angles.

Oh, sure. He knows that the sign painter got lost somewhere between the e and the l, but no one has ever corrected the mistake. And he is glad for this. There is some pleasure in imagining the angular architecture of this church, the masses that are celebrated there, the type of congregation that has chosen this name. A congregation interested in the perpendicular, the acute, the obtuse, the equilateral, in the intersection of lines, in beginnings and endings.

The doctrine of this church is based on the belief that when two lines intersect four angles are created. That these lines can extend forever without touching again. That the moment of intersection may be the only chance. That the lines, as they move away from each other, though, may for some reason stop, change direction, intersect again and again. That these intersections, these angles, these geometric shapes are what make up the church, the body of believers. Before too long, the first intersection is lost in a maze of lines and angles, and no one knows exactly where it all began.

Ryan Kutter

Chicken Scratch

I scribe letters in gravel and mud,
Words of impermanence and joy.

A colony of poets, pullets and hens,
Scrawl their own poems around me,

Bend their beaks to the ground
To see if they have it right.

Soon a Rhode Island Red steps over
To reckon what I've written.

She scratches my work away with Y tined toes,
invites the others to edit as well.

I concede the point, stray toward their stanzas

And clearly,
             unspeakably,
                           I meant this.

— Traverse County —

Gladys Field Carlson

Reflections in Memoriam

One by one the years flow by
Sweeping toward eternity.
We scarcely note the mounting toll
Until youth's gone and we are old.

One by one friends take their leave
While we remain on earth to grieve
The voices stilled, the empty places
That once were warm with smiling faces.

One by one, my thoughts restore
On sleepless nights, those gone before
Who wander back through memory's lane
And I am with them once again.

One by one the ties are broken,
One by one, the "good-byes" spoken
Until at last the tears I shed
Are for the living—not the dead.

— Wabasha County —

Jeanette Hinds

Open Mike Poetry in a Restaurant

(An Apro-POE Comment)

Napkined silver spins and clatters
    voices rise in bits and tatters
    speaking of the smallest matters
as the mike's so sudden screeching
    broadens to a yowl.

Then my voice becomes a bell
  spreading its unnoticed knell
  toward the backs of clientele
forking down their sliced tomatoes,
wading deep through mashed potatoes.

Verbs crash into meatloaf wall.
Ketchup-clogging cleats that crawl
free-verse heights get stuck and fall.
    Do I stand
    poem in hand,
speaking vacuums that I wrote—
clapper sticking in my throat?

Is this my offering of words
yeasted through each careful hour?
Poet's bread—joy to devour?
I've forgotten how to knead it
I've forgotten how to read it
    to a crowd who doesn't heed it
as it lies so pale and flat upon the page.

Worse, I feel a rising ire
toward the diners who retire.

Eyes averted with desire
    and a resolute endeavor
    now—now to leave or never—
what a world of solemn thought
    their monody compels
    as they slink out through the door.

And my poem from out their shadow
left behind upon the floor
shall be lifted nevermore.

Ronald Gower

The Way of Trout

How explain that
It must be this way
Unless it is only
In this way
To walk in beauty.

It is all ritual
And the crafted
Fly must be a
Perfect song
To walk in beauty.

The water is
A sheet of music
With no notes
But you must read
To walk in beauty.

A piece of water
Breaks, a note
Turns solid fire
Perfect music
As you walk in beauty.

Trout too catch fire
Sing, hook in lip
Send music up
The line and rod
To end in beauty.

— Wadena County —

Marlene Mattila Stoehr

Onion Tears

Evening. Nearly mealtime in our farm home.
My mother was carving remnants of Sunday's roast for hash.
One long ring on our wall telephone,
a call to Central on the party line.
I listened in. Everybody did.
It was this news I heard and had to tell:
"That was Mrs. Peterson. Ed just died."

Our neighbor, Ed Peterson, just died.
Settler farmers.
Our small farms were very near.
These parents shared the heartbreak
and the struggles of hard Depression years.
Pioneer Finnish families.
They neighbored. Sharing grownup secrets
children's ears were not to hear.

But Ed just died, and I,
not yet conscious of the unrelenting rules of death,
came to understand the strength of friendship that day.
I learned that some emotions
run too deep to be expressed in words.

"Ed just died."
My father heard me.
He sat a moment,
then without a word,
left his paper on the chair,
moved to the table,
and began to chop the onions for the hash.

Marta Hill

The Running of the Bulls into Staples

The big rigs chase
their drivers' cabs
across the prairie.
Down chutes of asphalt,
past sugar beets
and durum wheat,
tearing over
Red River bridges,
past grain bins
and elevators,
chased to truck stop
in Wadena.
Constantly guarding
against goring
brokers and dispatchers.
Running to and through Staples.
Running even while asleep
in cab-overs and conventionals.
Fuel stops stir
common language
of coffee and per mile.
Counting quarter million
miles like cash—
kissing days and suns and scenes
goodbye.
Pushing into morning

the big, ornery rig
chasing,
steered by
highway cowboys.

— **Waseca County** —

William Reichard

Encounter, Late

startled by the beauty of its form
headlights illuminating asphalt only

a second
                            then the buck
framed perfectly
                            delivered
from darkness into this moment
            frozen
                    midair

our eyes meet
                    creature to creature

we both know what's to come

shattering glass and metal torn
and I'm screaming more loudly
than I ever have before

the car's body stops but
my body's still moving
            the dashboard

                        the window
yanked back by the seat belt

he continues his flight
back into the void

I crawl from the totaled car
run breathlessly a mile up the hill
to my home

                the stars are cold
and hard
            and the night air sharp

in the ditch he finds a way
out of this world's darkness

Emma D. Babcock

Wind of the Matawan Prairie

O summer wind, blow gently
Across our prairie land;
Touch all the flowers lightly
That bend beneath your hand:

Blue iris in the meadows,
Wild phlox along the way …
In the early morning,
The scent of prairie hay.

Wind, now cease your moaning—
Give me a moment's rest!
Turn your wild weird sighing
Into a merry jest.

For, though we tame the prairie,
The wind we cannot tame,

And flowers blown too often
Can never be the same:

Blue iris in the meadows,
Wild phlox along the way ...
And, in the early morning,
The scent of prairie hay.

— Washington County —

Jorie Miller

From the Heavens

for Julie and Amara

All through the night the pains came to her.
Lightning and thunder passed over her house,
heavy rain ran down the gutters.
She took breaths, closed her eyes,
opened them—eager to let this night, this rain
help the child be born.
All night, all through the rain,
a woman labored.

All night a child rode waves of water, not an ocean,
but a storm in the middle of this nation.
The woman walked once to the porch,
put her face to the screen door and thought,
This moment is passing through me.
These are my hands, these are my pains.
There are stars falling behind those clouds.
There is no storm that lasts forever.

All night a woman labored until the water

outside her fell all the way through her.
And the lightning and thunder was inside
her and ripped an opening.
She opened. She flowed like a river.
And the child moved out of the waters
into air and calm.

— Watonwan County —

Stash Hempeck

Friends

Paul Wenstrom's leg,
stout and oakish
as his blacksmith father,
finds my meatless twig
just above the ankle.
They greet each other
in total surprise like
two ten-gauge shotguns
blasting next to our ears.
We both go down,
the first casualties
in our now lethal
Letterman's War
here on the football field.

But then our lizard brains
go into shock mode,
and the juice of adrenalin
spurts into our systems like
mist into a diesel engine.
It slows our senses,

allows us to talk calmly
about my new body shape,
and we marvel the lack of a crimson tide,
stare in awe at the jagged points
of the two snow-white teeth
poking through flesh.

Inside the ambulance,
Paul flexes the fingers
of his right hand,
waving them like
the white worms we once found
in bat droppings,
and marvels at how mine,
clenched tightly around his palm,
are still so full of color.

— Wilkin County —

Sharon Chmielarz

Cow, a Pastoral

She's wandered loose from pasture,
dropping her boa but keeping her spots.
Now she must rest. She's parked
her arse beside a country lane,
to study her shadow, doze in the sun
on a lovely, expansive late afternoon.
She ignores her teats, aching to be milked.
An old cow, wise beyond her rump.
There's grass to munch, that which she lies in.
Before nightfall the farmer will come,
geehawing her name with a git-on-home.
Her resumé, her udder.
She, who loved milk as a calf, is fated
to pass its peace on to the world.

Sharon Chmielarz

Headstones

They have to last. That's why
granite is the likely choice
for their composition. They have
to stand up to the Northern Plains,
its fierce summers, its scouring
winter wind and the earth
sinking under their foundations.
They have to be dutiful, loyal to
the name and dates inscribed
on their chests, good soldiers
though constant failures, unable
to convey any further correspondence.

— Winona County —

Loren Niemi

In River Towns

The white clapboard houses crowd the roadside,
their windows, whatever their number,
want only the river where
they see the promise of the far shore.

At night the lights from the tows
search their cupboards,
illuminate the pictures of loved ones, cross the ceiling
and steal away again.

When the pensioners' checks are cashed,
the old men raise a glass to quicksilver fish
not caught and to the rumble of the trains
making the juke box skip.

Emilio DeGrazia

Mississippi River Town

(Winona, Minnesota)

Here ancient time remains still.
While citizen-strangers in solitary streets
Are moved by roads leading away,
Life, liberty, and the pursuit of property
Trespass equally here.

And as the river treads water
Above local chemistries,
And carbon ghosts hover
Over passing dreams,
Wind's lofty singing endures.

Here the bluffs still hold their ground,
And water finds new ways
To be the same Old Man.

Even the elm, finally defunct,
Recalls in its browned bones
The once-upon-a-time woods,

And when the blackbird turns its head
Toward horizon of corn and sky,
Fences are an invisible blur.

Emilio DeGrazia

Weeds

(Thanks to Gerard Manley Hopkins)

The thistle and thorn, the ragweed dress
Shredded by hail and smattered by rain
Beworms the mud moiled in the plain
With loam cropped bare to the bone

So tongue is skull-numbed,
Dumb to Adam, red clay and words—

So let them be left,
Oh let them be left, the weeds
And the words,

The thistles and thorns, and Eve
On the leaf bristling with verse—
Oh let them be left, all wild and wet!
Long live the earth in her ragweed dress!

— **Wright County** —

H. L. Gordon

Dollars and Dimes

Dollars and dimes, dollars and dimes!
Ah! love is purchased with silver and gold,
And peace and pleasure are bought and sold,
And *friendship* is crying open and bold:
Dollars and dimes, dollars and dimes!

Dollars and dimes, dollars and dimes!
The hungry beggar is starving for bread;
He prays for the loan of a crust and a bed;
The rich man cries, with a shake of his head:
Dollars and dimes, dollars and dimes!

Dollars and dimes, dollars and dimes!
The belle, whose heart is longing to wed,
Tho' worth and virtue have often pled,
She lisps with a fashionable toss of the head:
Dollars and dimes, dollars and dimes!

Dollars and dimes, dollars and dimes!
The judge, enthroned in his sacred seat,
With never a face or heart to cheat,
Cries, holding the scales of "justice complete":
    Dollars and dimes, dollars and dimes!

Dollars and dimes, dollars and dimes!
This world is fleeting, prepare for the next;
The preacher can save your soul, perplexed,
But mark, he asks at the end of his text:
    Dollars and dimes, dollars and dimes!

Margaret Horsch Stevens

Grandmother's Wedding Gown

Today I took this wedding gown
From its accustomed place
And gazed upon a loveliness
Of taffeta and lace.

A hundred years ago it was
Grandmother's bridal dress
And the beginning of her life
Out in the wilderness.

But, somehow, this is more than just
A thing of tucks and seams;
I think Grandmother was the kind
Who stitched in all her dreams.

How often, when her days were dark,
Her dreams would reappear
To brighten up the commonplace
And help dispel her fear.

So, through the years, I keep this gown—
Much more than cloth and lace;
It lies, in memory of her,
In its accustomed place.

— Yellow Medicine —

David Pichaske

Teach Your Children Well

> *"and feed them on your dreams"*
> —*Crosby, Stills, Nash & Young*

Can tell you only what I have come to know:
clean, black cut of new-paved road
(always north and always uphill)
flanked by yellow beans and khaki corn;
behind, hollow moon dragging her sullen face
toward dark tangle of the Yellow Medicine River
(cottonwood, deer, fox, and pheasant);
ahead, flame of northern lights, aurora borealis,
and, always, firm distance of the pole star.

Florence Dacey

Two Poems from *Maynard Went this Way*

1.

Maynard doesn't exactly go
down the middle of the road
though sometimes he covers
twenty feet in a fairly straight,
as a country road goes, line,
in a kind of movement of his rump
that makes me wonder how he'll limp
when his skeleton starts to fade.

Maynard makes a pretty web as he goes,
dash to that rabbit by the fence,
plunge in soybeans,
down in the ditch,
straddle the line,
now it's left,
then to the right.

Maynard, the politician,
except his politics
are olfactory and all unfixed.

It's unclear if he leads or follows.
He wants to keep you company,
a strange ideology,
and if you leave this road
for deer trail, furrow, rock
or simple straying,
he's there, nearby,
as if he knew the way.

As if you did, too.

2.

Corn is high and near perfect this July
along Maynard's road, our walk.

He enters one dark narrow tunnel
and is lost to me.
Maynard hasn't read
of Terminator seeds,
genetically engineered,
of the killing of the soil
and our family farms,
won't wonder if these glossy leaves
and plush, tasseled ears
are part of that misguided scheme.

He'll wander in that lush shady forest.
He'll smell the earth, roots, falling kernels.
Heady, he'll emerge with corn pollen
on his black back, pale twists of life
on the rough ground of his body.

He'll carry them unthinking
and shake them off in time,
the perfect pollen
from the perfect corn.

Mildred B. Lee

Epilogue

Age speaks to age; and in this hour
Of man's triumphant mastery of power,
Of giant turbines, cataclysmic force,
What message from the age of ox and horse?

Only this message, vital to the race:
Man's nature is not changed by change of pace.
Still he will need the faith, the will to bear
The burdens of his time, and boldly dare
To serve on new frontiers the larger plan
For freedom in the brotherhood of man.

So we salute you, valiant pioneers;
May history tell of us as fair a tale
When in some future time these troubled years
Are long, long past. Let time unveil
Our city's glorious destiny and tell
That in our time we served, and served it well.

Epilogue

Jim Northrup

Dash Iskigamiziganing

Nimbiindaakoojige,
Ninga-naadoobi iwidi noopiming wayiiba
Aaniin apii waa-ozhiga'igeyan iwidi Gwaaba'iganing dash,
Mii bijiinag i'iw apii baadaajimowaad aandegwag dash,
Mii zhigwa oshki-ziigwang
Aaniin dash apane wenji-izhichigeyan i'iw dash,
Apane nimishoomisiban apane gii-izhichige dash,
Awenen wii-wiidookawik iskigamizigeyan dash,
Indanawemaaganigdog miinawaa dash, niwiijiwaagan dash,
Awenen waa-mawadisik iskigamizigeyan dash,
Awegwen iidog dash,
Aaniin dash apane wenji-izhichigeyan dash,
Ninijaanisag miinawaa dash, noozhishenyag miiniwaa dash, akina
Anishinaabeg niigaan igo ani-nitaa-iskigamizigewag dash,
Awegonen waa-aabajitooyan iwidi iskigamiziganing dash,
Ninga-indaabaji'aa asema dash, ininaatigoog dash, bagone-igan dash,
Negwaakwaanan dash, ziinibaakwadwaaboo dash, iskigamiziganaak dash,
Okaadakik dash, misan dash, iskigamigani-ishkode dash,
    zhingobaandag dash, dibaajimowinan dash
Mii iw
Mii sa iw

Contributors

Gordon Anderson (Sibley County)
Lee Assenmacher—Rochester (Olmsted County)
Emma D. Babcock—Matawan (Waseca County)
David Bengtson—Long Prairie (Todd County)
Doris Bergstrom—Pine River (Cass County)
Marlys Tennyson Binger—Minnetonka (Hennepin County)
Robert Bly—Minneapolis (Hennepin County)
Gary Boelhower—Duluth (St. Louis County)
Jane A. Bouma—Madison Lake (Blue Earth County)
Edward Reimer Brandt—Minneapolis (Hennepin County)
Ruth Brin—Minneapolis (Hennepin County)
Josephine Brower—St. Cloud (Stearns County)
Michael Dennis Browne—Minneapolis (Hennepin County)
    and Benedict (Hubbard County)
Philip S. Bryant—St. Peter (Blue Earth County)
Marjorie Buettner—Chisago City (Chisago County)
Robert E. Caldwell—Brook Park (Pine County)
Gladys Field Carlson—Wheaton (Traverse County)
Richard Carr—Minneapolis (Hennepin County)
Susan Stevens Chambers—Good Thunder (Blue Earth County)
Jean L. Childers—Eden Prairie (Hennepin County)
Sharon Chmielarz—Brooklyn Park (Hennepin County)
Patricia Conner—Cass Lake (Beltrami County)
Meredith Cook—Blue Earth (Faribault County)
Chet Corey—Bloomington (Hennepin County)
Florence Dacey—Cottonwood (Lyon County)
Philip Dacey—New York—Taught at Southwest Minnesota
    State University (Lyon County) for more than 30 years
Leo Dangel—Yankton, South Dakota—Emeritus Professor
    of English at Southwest Minnesota State University (Lyon
    County)
Frances March Davy—Shakopee (Scott County)
Emilio DeGrazia—Winona (Winona County)
Charmaine Pappas Donovan—Brainerd (Crow Wing County)
Alixa Doom—Le Sueur (Le Sueur County)
Inez Jane Dopp—Graceton (Lake of the Woods)
Claire van Breemen Downes—St. Cloud (Sherburne County)
James Elberling—Eagan (Dakota County)
Barbara Enright—Dassel (Meeker County)

Lorraine Powell Erickson—Pipestone (Pipestone County)
Angela Foster—Pine City (Pine County)
Kay Foy—Columbia Heights (Anoka County)
Rebecca Taylor Fremo—St. Peter (Nicollet County)
Margot Fortunato Galt—St. Paul (Ramsey County)
Larry Gavin—Faribault (Rice County)
Jane Graham George—Minnetonka (Hennepin County)
Marie Vogl Gery—Northfield (Rice County)
Diane Glancy—St. Paul (Ramsey County)
H.L. Gordon—Clearwater (Wright County)
Ron Gower—Good Thunder (Blue Earth County)
Vicki Graham—Morris (Stevens County)
Kay Grindland—Grand Marais (Cook County)
Laura L. Hansen—Little Falls (Morrison County)
Phebe Hanson—St. Paul (Ramsey County)
Sharon Harris—Park Rapids (Hubbard County)
Margaret Hasse—St. Paul (Ramsey County)
Mike Hazard—St. Paul (Ramsey County)
Stash Hempeck—Hendrum (Norman County)
Tom Hennen—St. Paul (Ramsey County)
Dennis Herschbach—Two Harbors (Lake County)
Annette Hermansen—Roseau (Roseau County)
Marta Hill—Crosby (Crow Wing County)
Jeanette Hinds—Rochester (Olmsted County and Edina
    (Hennepin County)
Bill Holm—Minneota (Lyon County) and Iceland
Winifred M. Hoppert—Windom (Cottonwood County)
Mary Willette Hughes—Waite Park (Stearns County)
Louis Jenkins—Duluth (St. Louis County)
Katharine Johnson—Cloquet (Carlton County)
Stephanie N. Johnson—Duluth (St. Louis County)
Coleen L. Johnston—Mazeppa (Goodhue Copunty)
Athena Kildegaard—Morris (Stevens County)
Scott King—Northfield (Rice County)
Evelyn Klein—Woodbury (Washington County)
Jeanne Showers Knoop—Togo (Itasca County)
Ryan Kutter—Grey Eagle (Todd County)
Bob La Fleur—Ponsford (Becker County)
Michael Lange—Nicollet (Pipestone County)
Anna Marie Larson—Mankato (Blue Earth)
Steven Lewis Larson—Starbuck (Pope County)

Ed-Bok Lee—Minneapolis (Hennepin County)
Mildred B. Lee—Granite Falls (Yellow Medicine County)
Jane Levin—Edina (Hennepin County)
Frances Lyksett—St. Paul (Ramsey County)
Freya Manfred—New Richmond, WI—Born and raised in
    Luverne (Rock County)
C. Mannheim—Apple Valley (Dakota County)
Marianne McNamara—St. Paul (Ramsey County)
Mrs. H.E.B M'Conkey—St. Paul (Ramsey County)
Bill Meissner—St. Cloud (Stearns County)
Jorie Miller—Oakdale (Washington County)
John Minczeski—Maplewood (Ramsey County)
Tara Moghadam—Breezy Point (Crow Wing County)
Loraine Schwanke Mueller—Tracy (Lyon County)
LouAnn Shepard Muhm—Park Rapids (Hubbard County)
Loren Niemi—Minneapolis (Hennepin County)
Jim Northrup—Sawyer (Carlton County)
Joe Paddock—Litchfield (Meeker County)
Nancy Paddock—Litchfield (Meeker County)
Roger Parish—Burnsville (Dakota County)
Thien-bao Thuc Phi—Minneapolis (Hennepin County)
David Pichaske—Granite Falls (Yellow Medicine County)
Karsten Piper—Fulda (Murray County)
Gordon Prickett—Aitkin (Aitkin County)
Matt Rasmussen—Robbinsdale (Hennepin County)
William Reichard—St. Paul (Ramsey County)
Ann Reid—Hutchinson (McLeod County)
Marcie R. Renden—Minneapolis (Hennepin County)
John Calvin Rezmerski—Mankato (Blue Earth County)
Mike Rollin—Minneapolis (Hennepin County)
Maxine Russell—Brainerd (Crow Wing County)
Edith Rylander—Grey Eagle (Todd County)
Anne M. Schauer—Kasson (Dodge County)
Candace Simar—Pequot Lakes (Crow Wing County)
Doris Lueth Stengel—Brainerd (Crow Wing County)
Margaret Horsch Stevens—Montrose (Wright County)
Marlene Mattila Stoehr—Shoreview (Ramsey County)
Joyce Sutphen—Chaska (Carver County)
Thom Tammaro—Moorhead (Clay County)
Yuko Taniguchi—Rochester (Olmsted County)
Edith Thompson—Houston (Houston County)

Janet Timmerman—Lake Wilson (Murray County)
Diego Vázquez, Jr.—St. Paul (Ramsey County)
Mark Vinz—Moorhead (Clay County)
Beverly Voldseth—Goodhue (Goodhue County)
Ruth Wahlberg—Two Harbors (Lake County)
Paul Walsh—Rochester (Olmsted County)
Connie Wanek—Duluth (St. Louis County)
Cary Waterman—St. Paul (Ramsey County)
Charles Waterman—St. Peter (Nicollet County), Kasota and
    Le Center (Le Sueur County)
David Wee—Northfield (Rice County)
Karen Herseth Wee—Northfield (Rice County)
Joan Wiesner—Brainerd (Crow Wing County)
Bonnie Ann Wolle—Truman (Martin County)
Chris York—St. Paul (Ramsey County)
Lloyd Young—Pine City (Pine County)

194

Acknowledgments

We have sometimes been unable to find lines that would let us identify or contact some of the poets represented here. We hope that they will forgive our compulsive need to present their work to you, and that perhaps you might be able to help us reconnect their Minnesota experiences with ours and yours, so we can give them complete and grateful acknowledgment. We thank all the poets whose work is included here, and also all the many poets whose fine work we were unable to include.

For various kinds of support of this project, we particularly thank Marilyn Bengtson, Robert Bly, Ed Brandt, Marcy Brekken, Susan Chambers, Meredith Cook, James Donovan, Ron Gower, Shelley Harrison, Mike Hazard, Bill Holm, Scott King, Anna Larson, Sherry Quan Lee, Mary Lou Marchand, Loonfeather Press, Joe Paddock, Jim Pearlman, David Pichaske, Lorna Rafness, Candace Simar, Mary Ellen Stolle, Nathan Vevea, Beverly Voldseth, Connie Wanek, and Suz Anne Wipperling.

"Elegy for the Last Pioneer" by Gordon Anderson first appeared in *Poets of Southwestern Minnesota*, Joe and Nancy Paddock, ed., Southwest Minnesota Arts and Humanities Council, 1977. Reprinted by permission of the editors.

"Wind of the Matawan Prairie" by Emma D. Babcock first appeared in *Minnesota Skyline*, League of Minnesota Poets, 1944.

"The Cows Nearly Make It" and "The Masses" from *Broken Lines* (Juniper Press, 2003) by David Bengtson.

"Her Spirit Rides the Wind" by Marlys Tennyson Binger first appeared in *The Moccasin*, League of Minnesota Poets, 1995.

"In a Boat on Big Stone Lake" by Robert Bly. *Unicorn Broadsheet Two*, 1968. Reprinted by permission of the author.

"The Minnesota Mississippi" by Edward Reimer Brandt first appeared in *The Moccasin*, League of Minnesota Poets, Spring 1983.

"Boiling Springs" from *Harvest: Collected Poems and Prayers* (Holy Cow! Press, 1999) by Ruth Brin.

"Lines to Jacob Brower" by Josephine Brower first appeared in *The Moccasin*, League of Minnesota Poets, Spring 1944.

"Evensong" from *You Won't Remember This* (Carnegie Mellon University Press, 1992) by Michael Dennis Browne. "Little Women" from *Smoke from the Fires* (Carnegie Mellon University Press, 1985) by Michael Dennis Browne.

"Remember" by Robert E. Caldwell first appeared in *The Moccasin*, League of Minnesota Poets, Summer 1940. "Submarine" by Robert E. Caldwell first appeared in *The Moccasin*, League of Minnesota Poets, Summer 1939.

"You Don't Have to Write Him a Sonnet" by Patricia Conner first appeared in *Dust & Fire: Annual Anthology of Women's Writing and Art*, Women's Studies and English Department, Bemidji State University.

"Midsummer Celebration" by Meredith Cook first appeared in *Painting with Words*, Artisans' Guild of Martin County, 1983.

"Pursuit" by Chet Corey first appeared in *Mankato Poetry Review*, May 1989. "We Travel Both Ways" by Chet Corey first appeared in *Kansas Quarterly*, Fall 1978.

"Two Poems from *Maynard Went this Way*" from *Maynard Went this Way* (Good Dog Productions, 2006) by Florence Dacey.

"Bagels and Brew" by Philip Dacey first appeared in *Slant*. "The Day's Menu" by Philip Dacey first appeared in *North American Review*.

"Stone Visions" from *The Crow on the Golden Arches* (Spoon River Poetry Press, 2004) by Leo Dangel.

"Perversity" by Frances March Davy first appeared in *The Moccasin*, League of Minnesota Poets, November 1937.

"Snapshot of an October Afternoon" by Charmaine Pappas Donovan first appeared in *From Ottertail and Thereabouts*, New York Mills Arts Retreat and Regional Cultural Center, January 1996.

"First Frost" by Inez Jane Dopp first appeared in *The Moccasin*, League of Minnesota Poets, Autumn 1959.

"House on the Bluff" by Claire van Breemen Downes first appeared in *River Images*, 2000. "A Wish for My 120th Birthday" by Claire van Breeman

Downes first appeared in *Thirty-Three Minnesota Poets*, Monica and Emilio DeGrazia, ed., Nodin Press, 2000.

"Ladies of the Northern Prairie" by Barbara Enright first appeared in *Poets of Southwestern Minnesota*, Joe and Nancy Paddock, ed., Southwest Minnesota Arts and Humanities Council, 1977. Reprinted by permission of the editors.

"Night in a Country Town Hospital" by Lorraine Powell Erickson first appeared in *Poets of Southwestern Minnesota*, Joe and Nancy Paddock, ed., Southwest Minnesota Arts and Humanities Council, 1977. Reprinted by permission of the editors.

"Farmer" by Angela Foster first appeared in *Otter Tail Review, Volume Two*.

"After Reading Tu Fu I Go Off to Catch Rough Fish in the Cannon River" and "Conversation with a Girl Sculpting a Fist: Faribault Learning Center" from *Least Resistence* (Red Dragonfly Press, 2007) by Larry Gavin.

"Swine Judging Dakota County Fair" by Jane Graham George first appeared in *Bedford Poets Anthology*, Privately Printed, 2007.

"March 21, 2005, The Shootings at Red Lake Reservation, Red Lake, Minnesota" by Diane Glancy first appeared in *Witness*.

"Dollars and Dimes" by H.L. Gordon first appeared in The *Poets and Poetry of Minnesota*, Mrs. W.J. Arnold, ed., S.P. Rounds, Book and Job Printer, 1864.

"Cinderella," "Sacred Heart," and "Wrestler" from *Why Still Dance* (Nodin Press, 2003) by Phebe Hanson.

"Life-Worn" by Sharon Harris first appeared in *Finding the Words: The Talking Stick, Volume 16*, Jackpine Writers' Bloc.

"Animal of the Earth" and "Out of Work More than a Year Still No One Answers My Letters of Application" from *Love for Other Things* (Dacotah Territory Press, 1993) by Tom Hennen.

"The Last Unlocking" and "Meditation on a Plow" from *My Mother's Keys* (Lone Oak Press, 2002) by Jeanette Hinds.

"A Circle of Pitchforks" from *The Dead Get By with Everything* (Milkweed Editions, 1990) by Bill Holm.

"A Taste for Reading" from *Quilt Pieces* (North Star Press of St. Cloud, Inc. 2001) by Mary Willette Hughes. "Late May" first appeared in *Encore: Prize Poems of the NFSPS 2007*.

"The First Farms" by Scott King first appeared in *Sidewalks*. "Peace Agreement" and "Restoring the Prairie" from *Leftover Ordinary* (Thistlewords Press, 2006) by Scott King.

"Scent of Leaves" by Evelyn Klein first appeared in *The Moccasin*, League of Minnesota Poets, 1998.

"The Penalty" by Jeanne Showers Knoop first appeared in *The Moccasin*, League of Minnesota Poets, Spring 1939.

"I Remember" by Michael Lange first appeared in *Voice*, Southwest Minnesota Arts and Humanities Council, January 1981.

"Emergency" and "Seasons of Hair" from *Real Karaoke People* (New Rivers Press, 2005) by Ed-Bok Lee.

"Epilogue" by Mildred B. Lee first appeared in *The Moccasin*, League of Minnesota Poets, Summer 1954.

"Devotion" by Jane Levin first appeared in *terrain.org*, 2008.

"Runestone Saga" by Frances Lyksett first appeared in *Minnesota Skyline*, League of Minnesota Poets, 1944.

"Blue Mound, Luverne, Minnesota" from *Swimming with a Hundred Year Old Snapping Turtle* (Red Dragonfly Press, 2008) by Freya Manfred. "The Glowing Brown Snails of Blueberry Lake" from *My Only Home* (Red Dragonfly Press, 2003) by Freya Manfred.

"Laundry Day" by Marianne McNamara first appeared in *Finding the Words: The Talking Stick, Volume 16*, Jackpine Writers' Bloc.

"The Temperance Watchman" by Mrs. H.E.B. M'Conkey first appeared in *The Poets and Poetry of Minnesota*, Mrs. W.J. Arnold, ed., S.P. Rounds, Book and Job Printer, 1864.

"After Our 30th Birthdays, My Wife and I Walk to the Center of the Lake" and "Hometown Widow Whose Laundry Never Gets Clean" from *The Sleepwalker's Son* (Ohio University Press, 1987) by Bill Meissner.

"From the Heavens" by Jorie Miller first appeared in *Mothering*, Winter 1994.

"The Fight" and "Thaw" from *Gravity* (Texas Tech University Press, 1991) by John Minczeski.

"Portrait of Pioneers" from *Petals of Roses Falling* (Xlibris Corp., 2008) by Loraine Schwanke Mueller.

"Offering" and "Shoveling Out" from *Breaking the Glass* (Loonfeather Press, 2008) by LouAnn Shepard Muhm.

"Ogichidaa" and "Shrinking Away" from *Walking the Rez Road* (Voyageur Press, 1995) by Jim Northrup.

"Frogs," "Kingsryder and McGraw," and "Waiting for Spring" from *Earth Tongues* (Milkweed Editions, 1985) by Joe Paddock.

"Hell's Gate" and "The Machine That Changed Winter" from *Trust the Wild Heart* (Red Dragonfly Press, 2006) by Nancy Paddock.

"What I Remember" by Roger Parish first appeared in *Bedford Poets Anthology*, Privately Printed, 2007.

"The Grandfathers" and "Teach Your Children Well" from *Exercises Against Retirement* (Spoon River Poetry Press, 1995) by David Pichaske.

"The Word *flat*" by Karsten Piper first appeared in *Prairie Poetry*, Spring 2008.

"This Place" from *Fingergun* (Kitchen Press, 2006) by Matt Rasmussen.

"The Fog" by Ann Reid first appeared in *Heartsong and Northstar Gold: Golden Anniversary Anthology of Poetry, League of Minnesota Poets 1934-1984*.

"grandmother walks" by Marcie R. Rendon first appeared in *Traces in Blood, Bone & Stone*, Loonfeather Press, 2006.

"Willmar at Night" from *An American Gallery* (Three Rivers Press, 1977) by John Calvin Rezmerski.

"16th Ave. sketches: Today's lovers" by Mike Rollin first appeared in *XCP: Streetnotes*, Winter 2008.

"Hangman's Tree" by Maxine Russell first appeared in *The Moccasin*, League of Minnesota Poets, 1995.

"Dream Warriors" from *Dancing Back the Cranes* (North Star Press of St. Cloud, Inc., 1993) by Edith Rylander. "Maple-Tapping Song" from *Hive Dancer* (Red Dragonfly Press, 2007) by Edith Rylander.

"Devil in the Details" by Candace Simar first appeared in *Talkin' Seventh Street Blues*, 2004.

"At the Clothesline" by Doris Lueth Stengel first appeared in *Finding the Words: The Talking Stick, Volume 16*, Jackpine Writers' Bloc.

"Grandmother's Wedding Gown" by Margaret Horsch Stevens first appeared in *The Moccasin*, League of Minnesota Poets, Winter 1958.

"Onion Tears" by Marlene Mattila Stoehr first appeared in *Finding the Words: The Talking Stick, Volume 16*, Jackpine Writers' Bloc.

"Bookmobile," "Comfort of the Sun," and "Homesteading" from *Coming Back to the Body* (Holy Cow! Press, 2000) by Joyce Sutphen.

"Blue Eyes," Foreign Wife Elegy," and "Ice Fishing" from *Foreign Wife Elegy* (Coffee House Press, 2004) by Yuko Taniguchi.

"Closing the Cabin" and "Thinking of Steinbeck and Charley" from *Minnesota Suite* (Spoon River Poetry Press, 1987, reprinted by Dacotah Territory Press, 1996) by Thom Tammaro.

"Afterward" by Edith Thompson first appeared in *The Moccasin*, League of Minnesota Poets, Summer 1939. "Dimenuendo" by Edith Thompson first appeared in *The Moccasin*, League of Minnesota Poets, May 1937.

"Homesteaders" from *Minnesota Gothic* (Milkweed Editions, 1992) by Mark Vinz. "Red River Valley" from *Long Distance* (Midwest Writers Publishing House, 2005) by Mark Vinz.

"When Grandpa Took Me Walking through the Town" from *Along the Craggy Shore* (Lakeside Printing, 1989) by Ruth Wahlberg.

"April" and "Duluth, Minnesota" from *Bonfire* (New Rivers Press, 1997) by Connie Wanek. "Ice Out" by Connie Wanek first appeared in *Great River Review*.

"First Thaw" and "Getting My Son" from *First Thaw* (Minnesota Writers' Publishing House, 1975) by Cary Waterman. "Raising Lambs" from *When I Looked Back You Were Gone* (Holy Cow! Press, 1992) by Cary Waterman.

"On Leaving a Poetry Reading at an Old Folks' Home" from *The Place* (Minnesota Writers' Publishing House, Booklet No. 8, 1977) by Charles Waterman.

"Loon" by David Wee first appeared in *Minnesota Poetry Calendar*, 2000.

"The Lesson" by Joan Weisner first appeared in *Brainerd Daily Dispatch*, 2003.

"Mixed Voices" from *Good Old Whasizname* (2005) by Lloyd Young.